OUT OF THE SHADOWS

Graham Ingram

Church Home Group Resources Ltd

OUT OF THE SHADOWS
Copyright © Graham Ingram 2008

All Rights Reserved

British Library Cataloguing in Publication Data

A catalogue record for this book is available from the British Library

ISBN 978 0 9532398 2 5

First Published 2008 by
Church Home Group Resources Limited
25 Castle Street, Hertford, Herts SG14 1HH, UK
T: +44 (0) 1992 515576
F: +44 (0) 1992 509625
E: info@CHGRL.org

Printed in Great Britain for
Church Home Group Resources Ltd

OUT OF THE SHADOWS

PREFACE

I didn't want to write this book. I was dragged kicking and screaming (not quite) by a good friend. He has been urging me to think about it for a year or two. I had every intention of standing my ground. I've tried writing books before with no success. But the subject of this book scared me. Over the last dozen years I've had enough innuendo, accusation, ridicule, rejection come my way to last me the rest of my days. For me to publish a book on homosexuality will only stir up muddy waters again, and probably lead to a fresh spate of criticism and the resultant pain. I've wanted this to be a healing period of my life, and a time for restoring some broken friendships.

But my friend challenged my prevarication with the question "Graham, if you don't write this book, who will?" He was pointing out my somewhat unusual position, in the spectrum of opinions, in the current fierce debate about homosexuality in the Christian Church. I am a convinced Evangelical; a Bible believing Christian of the more theologically conservative Calvinistic kind. I have been a pastor and Bible-teacher for more than forty years. But I am by sexual orientation gay, and for nearly two years I worked as an assistant pastor in a 'gay' church in California. I guess it does give me a somewhat different perspective on things.

Two years ago I stayed with my friend when he was visiting the farm he owns in South Africa. We'd met to discuss plans we had for building a property in Cape Town. Things were not going well; a lot of work was needed in re-designing the two residences involved. I went to bed worried and spent the night tossing and turning. My friend did the opposite. He is a very industrious, innovative guy who makes things happen. Instead of battling to sleep he stayed up for much of the night and produced a new plan, which was waiting for me on the breakfast table. Alongside was another piece of paper. He had spent part of the night drawing up an outline for the book he wanted me to write, chapter headings and all. Immediately I began thinking of excuses, the problem of finding an editor, publisher and finance. He had answers for all my protests even before I made them. He'd got me in a corner.

It was another eight months before I did anything. He had more or less convinced me that I ought at least to try. I was even feeling guilty for my unwillingness. But I was overwhelmed with inertia every time I thought of starting. It was only when I moved house, from Port Elizabeth to Cape Town, and had a period when no opportunities for ministry were coming my way, that boredom suddenly drove me to action. I had done all the cleaning in my small flat. There was no garden to cultivate. If I went shopping it tempted me to buy things I didn't really need. So in desperation I bought a notebook and began to scribble down some thoughts. Shortly afterwards I made a trip to England. I hate long flights, mainly because of the boredom. I had time that needed filling. And so the book began to develop.

I've been plagued with doubts all the way through the writing. There are issues on which I haven't come to final conclusions. How can you go into print without being sure of what you are writing? At the same time, in spite of what some people might think, I really am a convinced Evangelical Christian. I've sometimes said, half jokingly, that if I have a tombstone one day I would like the inscription to be, "He was a Gospel man". It means everything to me to be able to come to the end of life's journey and be able to say "I have fought the good fight, I have finished the race, I have kept the faith" (2 Timothy 4:7).

But the truth remains I am blessed or plagued with the fact that I am gay. That is part of the total package that makes me who I am. For most of my life I tried to deny it or hide it. When rumours forced me out of the closet I became ashamed that I had done nothing to try and help other people like myself. I was too concerned with hiding that part of my identity, and so preserving my reputation in the Christian community. Only when my reputation was seriously tarnished anyway, was I willing to do what God began to tell me to do, and share the message of his grace and love with gay people.

Out of that developed a new ministry, a very difficult one. It meant trying on the one hand to explain and interpret evangelical Christianity to gay people. Many of them see evangelicalism as the enemy. It's fundamentalism that's the chief culprit, but gay folk don't usually see the distinction. So their minds have become closed to a Biblical gospel. It meant on the other hand trying to explain to evangelical Christians, what it means to be gay, so that they may become more understanding, accepting and compassionate. In becoming that, they will be better able to portray the God who revealed himself in Jesus, the 'friend of publicans and sinners'.

I do not know how much change can be achieved in the Christian Church in the years immediately ahead. It's going to need a lot of courage to bring it about. But I do know that there has to be change, otherwise a large number of people who God loves will continue to be alienated from the Gospel. I feel a kinship with those people, of which I'm not ashamed. I understand the yearnings inside those wild, 'in your face', gay young people who refuse to apologise for who they are.

I understand those who are still standing in the shadows scared of being known for who they are. Some of them, from both groups, already know God but need to find him again. Most need to discover for the first time how much the gospel of Jesus is perfectly suited to them, with their longing to love and be loved. I dedicate this book to them, and to those straight Christians who are sticking their necks out to show the love of Jesus to all people. My friend is one of those.

Contents:

Chapter Four

Nature or Nurture?

Chapter Five

Gay Culture and Lifestyle

Chapter Six

"What does the Bible say?"

Chapter Seven — Change begins in the home

Chapter Eight — Where do we go from here?

Appendices

Three Studies for Church Home Groups

Chapter One - My Story

Life at School

For anyone who had eyes to see, it was obvious from my earliest years that I was homosexual in my orientation. In my pre-school and early school years I was playing 'house' with the little girls when I should have been kicking a ball with the boys. Hence the frequent catcalls of 'sissy Ingram' that followed me. No doubt there were other things in my mannerisms that invited the label. I certainly ran in a funny way. And neither then, nor now, could I throw a ball properly. In later years, even though I denied my homosexuality, I realised the importance of watching my body language and the pitch of my voice. I think I was fairly successful in dealing with some of those indications of my sexual orientation. I often felt that people were laughing at me, and that created its own body language. One of my colleagues once commented that he hated the way I walk around 'like a dog with its tail between its legs'.

By my early teens, when I should have started to take an interest in girls, I was in an all boys school. That I suppose helped to hide my growing attachment to boys. The fact that at that age I had become a 'fatty' helped to hide my total incompetence at sports of any kind. The title 'Sissy' had been replaced by 'Tubby' and later 'Elmer'. The latter was the one that stuck. It was pinned on me by one of the school bullies who had become my regular tormentor. He chose it because it sounded a bit like the girls name 'Alma'.

I had two budding 'love affairs' that I recall in those years. One was with a boy whose name I never discovered and to whom I never spoke. I was on holiday, with my parents, in Bournemouth and doing what I did on my holidays, train-spotting. At least it was a hobby boys did, and it is something you could do on your own. Each day I saw this 'god' on the opposite platform of Bournemouth railway station, also collecting engine numbers. He was in the centre of a circle of what appeared to be admiring friends. I can still recall him fairly clearly more than fifty years later. He was tall, with dark curly hair and wore a bright blue blazer. How much I wanted to be part of that circle and feel the glow of his presence.

There were others at school I was physically attracted to. I have a vivid mental picture of a guy called Freddy. He was at least a couple of years senior to me. He was an athlete who I often saw scantily clad. He must have worked out a great deal at a gym, because he had a beautiful sculptured torso. He was popular, macho and I think rather crude - a real jock. It all added to the attraction. I'm sure he despised me and I think hardly ever spoke to me. But I did have one genuine friend who was a bit of a hunk. It never ceased to surprise me that he wanted my friendship. I was always expecting him to reject me; so I never felt secure in the relationship. He was also fairly tall, with dark curly hair, blue eyes and a good body. He was genuinely beautiful. The friendship lasted throughout the remainder of my time at school and for some years afterwards, even though he joined the navy and spent years sailing around the world.

The last time I saw him was when he invited me to his wedding. He was thirty then, a huge fellow with a beard. The attraction had gone. But he was the only person with whom I ever had sexual intimacy, when we were at school. It was part of the horseplay that boys of that age get into. We sat next to each other in class on the back row. I would play a game of trying to grab his genitals and he would try and stop me. But I think he enjoyed it as much as I did. Sometimes he'd let me put my hand under his pleasingly rounded bum and keep it there for a

14

while. It's the only time in my life when I've been able to do what I so badly wanted to do, and get away with it.

College Years

I don't think I really fell in love until my college years, though the physical attraction to men was an established part of my life. I didn't think of myself as homosexual. There was so much ignorance of things sexual in my small town working class background in the early fifties that I wouldn't have known what the word meant, even less what such people did. Homosexual acts were illegal and therefore something only very bad people indulged in. I interpreted my feelings as a cry for close friendship. I was a desperately lonely teenager wanting intimacy.

But there was one moment when I had the opportunity for sex with a guy, and ran away from it. It was while I was doing compulsory national service in the Royal Air Force. I was in North Wales on a course organised by the RAF Chaplaincy Department. One afternoon I was wandering around the historic town of Conwy. When I went into a cafe for a cup of tea I was picked up by a University student, without realising what was happening. He suggested we walk around the town together. At one point he needed to visit a public toilet and I joined him. He soon made his intentions clear by urging me to join him in a stall. As the truth dawned I turned and ran, not only out of the public convenience, but up the road and out of sight, running as if the devil was on my tail! I had become a Christian shortly before and I took my faith very seriously. But my desire for intimacy with men had not gone away. Yet clearly I didn't connect it with what the student wanted to do.

In my years in Teacher Training College I became friendly with two brothers who attended the same church as me. I think I was a bit attracted to both of them. During college vacations I stayed with their family on one or two occasions. My mother had become very antagonistic to my new found faith and it was difficult going home. The brothers came from a large family. They were poor and lived in a small house, and as was common in those days in working-class households, beds had to be shared. I shared with the two boys. They worked different shifts, and so sometimes I slept with one and sometimes the other. I can still remember those delicious moments when I would wake in the night to find the younger brother's body entwined with mine. It was quite inadvertent on his part; he was a restless sleeper who thrashed around in the bed. I would lie very still, hardly daring to breathe, in case I woke him and ended the bliss.

Theological College

In theological college were several guys I felt passion for at different times. One of them would frequently put his arm round me, in a brotherly hug, and keep it there for some time. It was wonderful. I desperately needed the touch of men. But I always managed to spoil those friendships. The physical love, which could find no outlet, would turn to a possessiveness that they couldn't handle. Most of these guys, of course, were straight. But for a while I became friends with two guys, who I also felt attracted to, who I now realise were gay. I think we were all too spiritual to be able to recognise it or admit it. Like so many folk in those days, especially from evangelical backgrounds, we failed to interpret our feelings and desires correctly.

One of the others did confess a physical attraction to the third guy. I sometimes wonder what might have happened if either of them had shown signs of attraction to me. Would I have been able to resist this overwhelming longing for intimacy? After college that particular guy married, had two children, only subsequently to leave his wife for a man. It had been a 'girl next door' kind of marriage; two families in the same church who were very good friends. I suspect there might well have been pressure from the families for it to happen. Many Christians make the mistake of seeing marriage as a cure for

16

same sex desires. It is usually a disaster and very unfair to the heterosexual partner.

Sometimes several years would go by before 'I fell in love' again. Something that straight people find very hard to accept is that gay people do fall in love in exactly the same way as they do. It's the sex part that dominates the thinking of most straight Christians when they hear the word homosexual. Some gay people are very promiscuous and give priority to sexual fulfilment. But it's just the same with straight people. Dig deep enough and you find that what most gay people want, above everything else, is romance, intimacy and a real committed relationship, just like that found in a good heterosexual marriage. I enjoy romantic movies. I often sit with tears trickling down my face as I watch lovers embracing and kissing. The tears are for me. I want the same thing. It's hard living without sex. It's even harder living without intimacy.

Church Pastor

Once I got into pastoring a church I was sufficiently preoccupied, with the daily pressures of the ministry, not to be distracted too much by sexual temptation. During my college years, and those first years in the pastorate in south-east London, I was known for my zealous Christian life and my quest for holiness. I was strict and I was serious about achieving my goals. I was a great reader of the writings of the Puritans. I was an admirer of their theology and approach to life. They were hardly likely to incite me to perverted sexuality!

In theological college some of my fellow students disliked me because of my strict views on the Christian life. In the ten years between twenty and thirty years of age I didn't go to the cinema, not even once. I believed it was wrong for Christians, whatever the film. On one occasion I went to the theatre for an evening of Gilbert and Sullivan. Pretty harmless you'd think. I didn't think so. I went only because a young man in the local G & S Company had started attending my church. He wasn't yet a

Christian, so I could excuse his involvement in the theatre. I went to the show to strengthen my contact with him, and so win him for Christ. But I felt so uneasy about doing it that I crept into the theatre in the dark, five minutes after the show began. I was astonished, when the lights went up for the interval, to find myself sitting in a block of my own church folk!!

I was desperately lonely living on my own in the church manse, and so I hired a TV on a six month contract. I got rid of it within a few weeks. I told a leading member of the church, "I allowed the devil into my house through the back door but I've kicked him out through the front door". I didn't read novels in those days or any kind of magazine that could have polluted my mind. Of course I never went to pubs or clubs, or any kind of place where I might have met gay people. I doubt if I would have recognised a gay person if I'd met one; so great was my ignorance. I pursued God and my calling to preach his Word with fervour, and I had a good prayer life. I was associated with various holiness movements, including one that grew out of the teachings of the East African Revival, often called the Rwanda movement. It put a great emphasis on repentance from sin, and 'walking in the light' with one another, which led to much confession of sin.

The Baptism in the Holy Spirit

Early on in my ministry I was baptised in the Holy Spirit and became involved in the newly emerging Charismatic renewal. I say all this to emphasise that I left few, if any, doors open through which I could have been tempted by homosexual thoughts or influence. But it didn't stop me being sexually attracted to men. Among folk in the church that I got closer to, was a young man of my age, who I'm going to call Rob. He was very different from me, sporty, somewhat macho, a regular South London lad. The initiatives for friendship came from him. He obviously liked my company and was keen to know more about God. Eventually I conducted his marriage to a girl from the congregation. It was a relief for me to do it because the girl had shown clear signs of interest in me. I think she may have married him on the rebound after I made it clear I wasn't interested. Even as she walked down the aisle I got the distinct feeling she was still interested. Their marriage didn't last.

It's been one of the hazards of my ministerial life that I've been pursued by good women, who seemed to think I was the answer to their prayers. I think it was my zealous preaching rather than good looks that attracted them! To digress before coming back to Rob: during my five years of ministry in London I met several girls, while on Christian holiday tours (Yes - I even had Christian holidays!!), who became friends for a while, mainly through letters. I was lonely, and I knew ministers ought to be married, so I was hopeful that something might develop. But something just didn't click when we met. I went to visit one of the girls in Scotland. She was waiting for me when I arrived by bus, dressed up 'to the nines', and her face showed far too much eagerness. I froze. There was no way I could even hold her hand.

A year or two later I tried again with a nurse who was a really lovely girl, and a fine Christian. She would have made an ideal wife for a minister. She told friends of mine that she was strongly attracted to me. I knew there was no future in it, though at that stage of my life I didn't understand why. But I had come to realise that it was very unlikely I would ever marry and I decided to drop the idea of a serious relationship with the opposite sex. It was 'unnatural' for me. That's one of the problems interpreting passages like Romans 1, where homosexual acts are condemned as unnatural. Unnatural can depend on where you are coming from. For me it was very natural to be attracted to a man.

So back to Rob: we became good friends and as part of that friendship I used to go and watch him play football on Saturday afternoons. I went whatever the weather. I was in danger of freezing to death standing on the touchline in winter. But I can still remember the chief reasons I was so dedicated. He had great legs!

Lusaka Baptist Church

Somewhere in the middle of my five years in south-east London God began to speak to me about foreign missions, particularly Africa. I had always thanked God that I wasn't called to foreign fields. I suppose it was part of the insecurity of my growing years that I had little desire for adventure. Darkest Africa was a forbidding thought. So it was an enormous step for me to respond to God's call, and leave my homeland for the heart of a strange continent where I knew only one person. I also went without any guarantee of financial support.

The small Baptist church that called me, in Lusaka, Zambia, had only seven members left. I had no support from a missionary society, only the local congregation. All those seven members left the country in my first year. So I had a building and not much more. But the nearly eight years that followed were amongst the most fruitful and exciting of my Christian ministry. In fact they were wonderful. Hundreds of African young people came to Christ and were equipped for Christian service. Today many of them are in strategic positions in the church life, business life and political life of that nation.

There was little to tempt me sexually in Lusaka. I was busy, fulfilled and somewhat cut off from the culture of the western world. The drive-in-cinema was the only place to go for entertainment. TV was mainly local stuff and not very good. There was no obvious gay community. It would have been dealt with pretty severely if it revealed itself. But with little to do for relaxation I did start reading novels again. It was while reading an Arthur Hailey crime novel, the story built around a bank theft, that I finally realised why I was 'different'. There was a character in the book who got raped in prison. The act was described in some detail. To my horror I found myself identifying with it, and realised what my problem was.

I was in no doubt about it. It never occurred to me that there might be any remedy, apart from a determined attempt to stamp out any evidence and try and blot it out of my consciousness. I went through my journals from when I started writing in my late teens. My 'secret' was in fact very obvious in some of my comments, particularly in my college days when I was in love. It read like a school girl in a spin because the boyfriend was being cool to her. I struck out everything that could be a give away and tore out a lot of pages. But it was much harder to obliterate it from my mind.

Whenever I experienced some special touch from God in my life, I would be able to keep my thoughts under control for a while. But unfortunately life has its spiritual downs as well as ups. And then I would begin to fantasise about men again. I didn't masturbate because, astonishing as it may seem, I didn't know how! A young American came to stay with me once, on a short-term mission outreach. He was extremely good looking and with a gym-pumped physique which he bared for most of the time. I could hardly eat my food as he sat bare-chested at the table. I was so scared of the way my feelings and mind were running riot that I developed an antipathy towards him to protect myself.

Eventually I asked him to leave. He couldn't work out why. There was no legitimate way I could explain what was going on. But getting rid of him didn't solve the problem. The memories of that body remained. I fell seriously in love with someone in the church who was also very good looking and enjoyed my company. He was straight, there was no possibility of anything coming of it, and my possessiveness harmed the friendship.

Cape Town

After Zambia, it was Cape Town, South Africa. That was a scary challenge in itself and required a big step of faith. It was still the dark days of apartheid and I knew that at some point I would have to challenge the system. That was a daunting thought in itself, particularly as I was pastoring a conservative white Baptist Church. Anyone who challenged apartheid in that kind of church was usually regarded as a crypto-Communist. As a non-South African pastor I was also watched by the security police. There were some difficult times. But life and ministry was rewarding.

Over the years I saw, and was part of, some amazing changes in the church and nation. Later on I started a new church that was a direct result of a strong work of the Spirit, the nearest thing to Revival I have experienced. It grew rapidly to about fifteen hundred people; hundreds were converted and baptised. I was at the peak of my ministry and had become widely known, and generally well thought of, in the country. South Africa was now my home. There was no great vacuum in my life. I had a large circle of friends, some of them very close friends who loved me and were committed to me. I had a church full of young people, many of them very good-looking, sun-kissed South Africans. Their love, respect, and friendship did a great deal to fill that inner yearning. We were a church that did a lot of hugging, and being hugged by these gorgeous young men certainly eased the pain!

I even began to come out of the closet, somewhat unconsciously. Until the time of starting the new church I had remained reasonably conservative in my image and dress. I often wore trendy suits and ties but at least I dressed formally. The new church was radically different, part of the emergence of independent charismatic churches world-wide. We had a particular emphasis on the importance of the Biblical doctrine of Grace, as a teaching and as a life-style, free from legalism. I wanted to win the masses of young people who were fed up with religion and church formalism. Like every leader I needed to model what I was teaching. But it also gave me an excuse for dressing like I'd always wanted to dress, hipster-jeans, bright shirts or T-shirts; sometimes colourful waistcoats or braces.

Stories began to spread about the amazing transformation. Though never very conservative in dress, for many Christians I had been the pillar of Calvinistic Evangelicalism in Cape Town. A considerable number of students from the very conservative Bible Institute, and an even more conservative Holiness college associated with the Africa Evangelistic Band, sat under my ministry in the Baptist Church. Some of them have claimed in later years that I was the one who taught them how to preach. A visitor who had known me and seen me in both churches, commented that if the Graham Ingram now revealed in the new church was the real me, then it must have been terrible having to project a very different image for all those years. The true me was beginning to emerge, but most people didn't associate it with my sexual orientation, because it was part of something happening on a wider level in the new church culture.

But in all other respects I was treading the same path as I had for years, trying to pretend I wasn't gay and serving God to the best of my ability. The Holy Spirit was moving powerfully in our church, to some extent because of what I was experiencing in my own life. I was at the height of my preaching powers and God was moving Sunday after Sunday in the services. I had liberalised some of my attitudes, like most Christians in recent years, and was probably watching some movies and TV programmes that I might have been better off not watching; and I continued to battle with my thought life. But there was nothing worse than that.

I had no connection or association with the gay community and I was not pursuing a gay lifestyle. But I continued to become emotionally involved with men in the congregation, or men with whom I worked, though they didn't know it. It was painful and usually caused stress in relationships, even though I constantly curbed my desires. But on one occasion it nearly went further than that. I was sitting in the restaurant car of an excursion train travelling from Cape Town to Franschoek, a beautiful resort in the Winelands. I noticed a good looking guy wearing a stunning shirt. He and his shirt were both very sexy, and I was sure he was gay. I positioned myself so that I could watch him, hopefully without being noticed. But he did notice and later asked if he could join me at my table. I was both excited and scared. He told me right out that he was gay and did his best to shock me out of the closet. He pointed to an older man and told me that he was his lover. I felt very awkward but the same time every part of me was tingling with desire, because I was so close to something that inwardly I wanted. He gave me his card and invited me to dinner. He left it to me to phone him if I wanted to go. Did I want to go! I kept the card on my dressing table for several months, longing to ring him, but petrified of what it might lead to. I even persuaded a woman in the church to make me a shirt exactly like the one he had been wearing. I've still got it. I think it was only the certainty I had that I would be found out, and have to leave the ministry, that stopped me making that phone call.

I think my colleagues were starting to get suspicious. A number of openly gay people came to the church and though I didn't encourage them, nor did I deal with them in the way some of the staff might have liked. I made a mistake one day. One of the younger staff members liked to take a swim during his lunch break, in a pool which was part of our office complex. Sometimes he would work at his desk afterwards still wearing his speedos. It annoyed me. It was taking our relaxed style too far. I ought to have come down on it. It wasn't fair to people visiting the offices. But I was also annoyed because it put pressure on me in my own battle. The guy concerned had a great body. I usually tried to avoid looking directly at him. But one day, when I went into his office, I decided to embarrass him by looking directly at him and giving him a suggestive smile. He blushed and asked me what it was all about. I'm pretty sure that I gave the game away that day, and that incident became evidence in a case later built up against me. My life started to become very complicated. Career wise I was still riding on the crest of a wave.

Resignation and Rumour

But then things began to change. I decided to resign and found myself unemployed for a period of time. There was no scandal, no wrongdoing on my part, but the details are not relevant to the purpose of this book. I believe serious wrong was done against me by certain leaders from outside my church, but I have no desire to harm the people concerned. It is water long under the bridge.

I went back to England for several months but my heart was still in Cape Town, and I returned the following year. I came back with the intention of exercising an itinerant ministry; but circumstances led me into church planting again. I was involved in planting three churches over the next few years.

This was seen as a threat by the new leadership of my old church. A period of dispute began between the group of churches to which I was affiliated, and a new grouping to which my old church now belonged. The leaders of both groups were concerned about the 'bad blood', and felt we needed to deal with it. A number of us met together one morning, in the beautiful Kirstenbosch Gardens, to try and sort it out.

The chairman appealed to both sides to stop bad-mouthing each other, and made reference to a number of the accusations being made. Suddenly he said, "And people must stop saying Graham Ingram is gay". A shock went through my body. For a second I thought it was a sick joke. This was the first time I had ever heard it said publicly by people who were my friends. In spite of all I've written so far, I was still trying to convince myself that I would never have to deal with that question.

That evening I went to play Scrabble with a couple of older women friends; something I did regularly. The two were very fine women, who loved me and cared for me in so many practical ways. Sometimes I would share my heart with them, knowing they were utterly trustworthy. They noticed that night that I was looking very sad, and asked me why. When I told them they showed no surprise. I realised that they had already heard these rumours and they told me that they believed them to be widespread.

For several months I was in a period of shock. It didn't matter that the group of ministers, of which I was a part, took measures to defend my reputation. They tried to get apologies from the leaders who had played some part in the rumours spreading. What had been said couldn't be taken back. It was going to affect my life deeply and for a long time to come. One of the pastors of my former church visited me one day. Afterwards he told others that he was shocked by the pain in my eyes.

Some months after the Kirstenbosch meeting, I was sitting by a lake near my home. It was my favourite place for prayer times. But I wasn't in normal praying mood. Shock was beginning to turn to anger, and I started shouting at God that he had allowed all this happen. "God, how could you let them do this, how could you let them take away my reputation? I have done my best to serve you all these years".

A conversation followed that was as real, if not more so, as any human conversation I'd ever had. "My Son made himself of no reputation", the Lord said. He then reminded me how Jesus had been called a blasphemer, was described as demon-possessed, a glutton and drunkard, and how they crucified him as a common criminal. (As Jesus was an unmarried man over the age of 30 it is highly likely some suggested other things). He reminded me of the way Paul's converts deserted him, and how his ministry was undermined by vicious rumours from envious rivals. Then he reminded me that there were plenty of other things people could say about me if they knew all he knew. "All right, Lord. I quit complaining while I'm still winning. You know too much!!" I repented of my attitudes. And as I did the Spirit began to stir me in worship and praise to God, for allowing me to feel some very small part of what Jesus, and all his true followers, have experienced throughout the ages.

But God hadn't finished. He reminded me that even though there might be a vicious motive behind the rumours, the rumours were not themselves false. I am gay, and God had known that all the time, and it had made no difference to his acceptance of me, and his love and care for me. A great load began to lift. Why was I lying to myself and to God?

As over the months the pain began to diminish I started to examine my life and circumstances in the light of what had happened. I sensed that life would never be the same again. Even if the rumours diminished, there would always be the fear that they would re-occur. This kind of rumour is virtually never lived down. Whether it was true or false it would have plagued me the rest of my life. In admitting the truth I was free. I had actually harmed myself a great deal by trying to suppress for so many years what I knew to be true. I had to bring it out, move out of the shadows, and take a good look at it, and come to terms with what it meant.

Chapter Two - The Story Continued

Facing Reality

Many evangelical Christians will say that I should not have explored my homosexual tendencies. I should have rejected them immediately as being inconsistent with Christian faith. I should then have asked for help from one of the Christian ministries that exist for people like me.

I am sure that for some people these ministries do a good job. But I don't think it entered my head at that time. The only choice I saw before me was to go on pretending I wasn't gay, as I had done for more than twenty-five years, or face up to the reality and try to understand it. I was probably unaware that there were ministries that claimed that homosexuals could be 'healed'. I certainly wasn't aware of such ministries in South Africa.

I had a pretty good idea of what would happen if I went to some of my colleagues and asked for help. They would have got together a group of folk experienced in so called 'deliverance ministry'. They would have laid hands on me, and for as long as it took, done battle with the demons inside of me. I believe there are times when we are called on to cast out demons in the name of the Lord, as Jesus himself did. But too often deliverance ministry has become a cure-all for the sins and failings of the Christian life.

A friend told me of a woman, in his home group, who had

confessed to the problem of lying and queried whether she needed deliverance ministry. "What should I do about my problem", she wailed. "Stop it" was my friend's common-sense and Biblical advice. I had no confidence that this kind of ministry would do me any good. I had no sense at all that my problem was caused by specific demon activity. Same-sex attraction had always been a part of me, as opposite-sex attraction is normal to other people. I had never known anything else. And as I was by then in my fifties it seemed highly unlikely that I could suddenly become another person psychologically; because that is what it would have required.

The evangelical preacher and writer Tony Campolo in his book *"Was Jesus a moderate?"* comments on the lack of evidence for believing that a homosexual can change his/her orientation. He goes on: "Some of my evangelical friends refuse even to consider the empirical evidence. They want to believe that if homosexuals will only repent and seek counselling, all will be well. They just don't get it. People can repent of what they do, but they cannot repent of who they are. Being homosexual is not just a bad habit that can be broken. It is an essential part of the identity of some of our brothers and sisters."

Mel White tells the story of his own struggle with his sexual orientation in his book *"Stranger at the Gate".* Born in the Pacific north-west of the USA he was converted to Christ at an early age and nurtured in strong evangelical churches. A leader in Youth for Christ in his region in his early adult years, and later an evangelical pastor, he became widely known as a preacher, journalist, author and film-maker. He lectured at Fuller, one of the great evangelical seminaries of the world. He was a ghost-writer and speech-writer for people like Billy Graham, Francis Schaeffer, W.A. Criswell, and right-wing fundamentalists like Pat Robertson, Jerry Falwell and Oliver North. He was a man of impeccable evangelical and conservative credentials.

But from early years he became aware of same-sex attraction. It was antithetical to everything he believed. He hated himself because of it. He tried just about everything possible to find a cure; prayer and fasting, anointing with oil for healing, exorcism rites performed by Protestants and Catholics, aversion therapy - which jolted his body with electricity every time he felt stimulated by photos of men. For a time, chemical treatments left him drugged and barely coherent. Mel desperately wanted not to be gay. He even got married thinking that might solve the problem. But in his forties he gave up the attempts to become a person he was not. He faced reality. It meant divorcing his wife. It's interesting that she wrote the forward to his book, supporting him in what he had done.

Gay Churches

It was never an option for me to go back to where I had been for twenty-five years, trying to live in denial. Some of my Christian friends had long-suspected I was gay; more and more were coming to believe it. But they would have preferred that I didn't 'announce it'. They would have been happier if we had all carried on pretending. "Don't ask, don't tell", to quote President Bill Clinton's solution for dealing with gays in the US military. But that policy had done immense harm to me over the years, creating tension, fear and low self-esteem. Even if I decided later that radical spiritual surgery was required, I needed first to understand more about the real me, and get to know some people who shared my problem. It was very lonely being gay and an evangelical Christian leader, even though I knew there must be others like me. But where did I begin?

In Apartheid South-Africa there was very strict government censorship of all newspapers, books and films. Nelson Mandela could not be quoted, or his photograph published in newspapers or magazines. There was a strangle-hold on everything regarded as politically or sexually deviant. So in the period I am describing, no literature or film describing or depicting homosexual acts was allowed. Homosexual acts were a serious criminal offence and so any corporate activity of gay people had to be undercover. Things were just beginning to change at the time I was going through my own self-discovery.

I had already noticed that one particular chain of book-stores was openly displaying gay literature, including a locally produced magazine called Exit. So my first act of exploration was to buy a copy, with much nervousness as I handed my money across the counter whilst furtively looking over my shoulder. It was only as I handed over the money that I realised the man assisting me had been in my congregation some years before, but he didn't seem to recognise me. Maybe God blinded his eyes at that moment!

Along with a mixture of soft-porn pictures, news of local gay life and serious articles on the AIDS scourge, there were adverts for gay-related functions in different cities and towns of South Africa. I was intrigued to find several advertisements for churches. I was aware that there were so called gay-churches in the US. I had walked past one when visiting Los Angeles, even stopping for a moment to study the notice board with a degree of curiosity mixed, I confess, with some excitement. I was sure it couldn't be a real Christian church but that didn't stop the fascination.

I had not expected to find such churches existed in conservative South Africa. The great majority of churches in South Africa were either evangelical, conservative or at least orthodox. Few reflected the theological liberalism of Europe. One advert for a church in Pretoria particularly caught my eye. Readers were invited to ring a number for confidential help. I liked the way it was put; caring, sensitive, spiritual, Christ-centred. I rang - but not without first having worked out a strategy. No name, address, or phone number would be given, or any information that could lead to me being identified.

It was the first of a number of conversations I had with Roger, a gay Christian man who worked at the University of South Africa. He respected my desire for anonymity. I used a pseudonym, and the address of an empty house near mine. He wrote me a number of long letters in which he explained how he reconciled his sexual preference and practice to orthodox Christian teaching. He had in fact come to a personal commitment to Christ through the gay congregation of which he was a member. Roger was clearly an intelligent and thoughtful man who put his arguments well, but they were not totally convincing to a died-in-the-wool evangelical like me. But they did help me to see that there were some serious weaknesses in traditional evangelical thinking on this issue.

A New Direction?

The months went by. I was reading more and more: history, theology, ethics, romance, and about the enormous effects of AIDS on the gay community. Many of the gay movies beginning to appear on TV had AIDS-related themes. I was also praying a great deal. During my quiet times, spent by a lagoon near my home, I became more aware of my responsibility towards others like myself.

For years my only concern had been to avoid detection and to protect my reputation. But now I was troubled by the thought of the folk who'd come to me, their pastor, to share their secrets and find help. They were nearly always very nervous, sometimes sweating, fearing that I might reject them or expose them. There was the married missionary who had thought that marriage and fatherhood would solve his problem, but it hadn't. There was the young woman, the daughter of a very conservative pastor, who was clearly a Christian but convinced that she was damned because she could not break the practices of years. I've often wondered what happened to her. She was in despair, near suicidal. There was the young church leader who had been 'delivered' through one of the ex-gay courses but then found it hadn't worked. There was a guy struggling to keep a marriage together, while leading a double life. There was a married doctor who badly needed my help, but at the last minute backed off from telling me his story because he didn't trust me enough.

I only found that out years later. I was, I believe, gentle and understanding with all of them, but I did little more than spout platitudes, because I was too scared of giving myself away. Now I was facing the question of what I was going to do in the future, having been outed myself, though I was still arguing the issue. Clearly I had a responsibility towards these struggling, often frightened, children of God who had gone through a great deal more rejection and suffering than I had.

A trip to America proved to be a very important turning point. It had been planned for some time that I would accompany a group of South African Vineyard Christian Fellowship leaders to John Wimber's annual ministry conference in Anaheim, California. I planned to visit friends in Britain, America and Canada both before and after the conference. It was a golden opportunity to explore more, to visit churches where I could meet gay Christians. But how would I find them?

I wrote to Roger asking for suggestions. There was no immediate reply for a number of reasons. It was only on the day before I left that I got an answer. Knowing that it was too late for ordinary mail Roger had faxed a letter to a gay friend in Cape Town, and arranged for me to pick it up on the way to the airport. Only when I was settled on the flight to London did I have time to read it. What he wrote hit me between the eyes. Previously Roger had answered questions, given advice, but never been provocative. By this time he knew I was a preacher and knew I was soon to terminate my existing ministry, with nothing yet determined for the future.

He challenged me to use this opportunity to change direction and use my gifts to reach and serve the gay community. He suggested I make a completely fresh start and do it in the USA where there were large identifiable gay communities. He was also aware of how difficult it would be coming out in Cape Town, struggling with misunderstanding and opposition, and beginning a new ministry in a hostile environment.

I was shocked and shaken by the suggestion. But I breathed a sigh of relief as I remembered that he still didn't know my real identity and how to find where I lived. It was easy to terminate the contact and that would make an end of the matter. But even as I relaxed again, I had another of those unusual, and at first rather scary conversations with God. Conversations of this kind are rare for me, and there was a time in my life when theologically I would have rejected the idea. I'm not talking about audible voices, but thoughts and words coming into the mind with a clarity and immediacy that have the imprint of the Holy Spirit. Though not common with me, there are many examples in Scripture. They must, of course, be tested by Scripture but the Christian who closes his mind to such possibilities is in real danger of quenching the Holy Spirit, and missing some of the most important direction that can ever come from God.

Reaching Gay People for Christ

It seemed that God was picking up on the conversation we'd had a few months earlier, by the lagoon. To my first rejection of Roger's suggestion, God suddenly said, "But why not?" "Why not, God? You know why not. Isn't it obvious? He wants me to put my head on the chopping block by going to work with folk who most of your children think deserve your judgement not your grace." "But don't I care about the salvation of gay people like I care for all humankind? And if someone like you isn't going to tell them of my love, who else is? Didn't I call you years ago to leave your homeland and cross cultural boundaries with the Gospel?"

I suddenly realised what a huge mission field there is out there of unreached gay people who have been made to feel alienated from God. But they were a people no longer unreachable because, unlike the past when gays were closeted and almost invisible, they were now identifiable in almost every city of the world - in gay ghettos or villages, gay bars and restaurants, gay shops, gay theatres, gay churches, gay sports clubs, gay football teams, and gay pride parades and festivals.

Cities like London, Manchester, San Francisco, Los Angeles, New York have large numbers of gay people forming sometimes as much as 20% or more of the population. In some places like West Hollywood, the Castro area of San Francisco, Provincetown on Cape Cod, Key West and Miami Beach in Florida, Soho in London, and Brighton on the south coast of England, there are so many gay people it is possible to go there and observe a microcosm of gay life. Almost every second person seems to be gay in some areas. That makes it so much easier to reach them for Christ.

As the picture began to widen in my mind, and as a bit of the shock began to wear off, I suddenly started to laugh. It would probably have developed into quite a loud belly laugh but for the looks of my fellow passengers. "But God you really are amazing", I said. "You are being very radical if I'm hearing you correctly." "You wouldn't be saved if I wasn't so radical. The most radical thing I ever did was to send my Son to the Cross".

At that moment I knew something very decisive was happening. I was catching a different view of the heart and mind of God, different from the one I often got from my evangelical culture and background; that very respectable middle class view of the Christian life which so many of us take as being the genuine article, a safe and sanitised view of things that has very little space for risk. But I also knew that I had to be very careful. This kind of guidance can easily be counterfeited. The Devil can come as an angel of light. I knew what my evangelical friends would make of it, if I claimed this experience as my guidance for making such a big decision.

So I said "All right God. I'm listening and I'm ready to follow if it's really you speaking. But on this one you are going to have to underline it again and again. I'll go through any doors that you clearly open. But I'm not going to push them. I stop when the doors stop opening."

I got off the plane at Heathrow and walked to the W H Smith's kiosk to buy a newspaper. On the racks I saw, and then bought, a copy of a magazine called *"The Gay Times"*. Again I found churches listed. The first was in Bournemouth, my first destination in England. The second was in south London where I was going the following week. Coincidence?

The Metropolitan Community Church

I was about as terrified as some of the folk who had been to me for counselling, when I walked around the streets of Pokesdown in East Bournemouth, the following Sunday morning. I walked around the block where the Metropolitan Community Church building was situated about six times before I went in. By then the service was already underway.

I got two immediate surprises. First - the smallish congregation looked very ordinary and un-intimidating. The much bigger surprise was the recognition that the Holy Spirit was also present. I could see it in the young minister's face as he led the congregation in a hearty singing of "All things bright and beautiful." I could hear it in the prayers as the congregation was given opportunity to share in open ministry. There was a humility, a reality, an awareness of God's love and grace that touched me. I didn't know how to explain it.

I knew that most of my evangelical friends would say I was deceived. But here in this congregation of people who were pretty obviously homosexuals, and probably practising homosexuals, the Holy Spirit was present. I am fully aware of the power of spiritual deception but I also know the evidences of the Holy Spirit's presence. There was love, joy, peace amongst these folk.

Since then I have been in gay churches where the Holy Spirit was not obviously present, where liberal theology and worse predominated. I am no longer involved on a regular basis with gay churches. I wish they didn't have to exist. I see them at best as a temporary expedient. But there is no doubt in my mind that there are many practising gay Christians who are indwelt, even filled, by the Holy Spirit.

Over the last few years I have preached quite a few times in a church in southern California where the pastor and ninety per cent of the congregation is gay. It is not affiliated to any grouping of gay churches. It is firmly Evangelical and Charismatic, the members born again. The worship is some of the best I've experienced anywhere; the preaching often powerful. The Bible studies and prayer meetings are like those of any good evangelical church and when I preach there I preach the same kind of message as I preach anywhere else, and it is received warmly. They have adopted me as their church missionary and, as well as praying for me, have regularly given financial help - even though I have been working amongst black University students in South Africa over these years, and have had little contact with the gay community.

How do I explain that the Holy Spirit is with such people? In one way I can't. It runs contrary to my life-long theological convictions. I wouldn't for a moment conceive that the Holy Spirit would be present in a congregation of practising adulterers or professional bank robbers. But I have experienced the presence and power of God amongst gay Christians.

I do not build my theology or my interpretation of Scripture on experience. I know that God is very gracious and because of that sometimes appears to do strange things. But I have to say that if our interpretation of Scripture, on the issue of homosexuality, is correct - it has to take cognisance of experience. There has to be some harmony between the two. The traditional interpretation of Scripture on this issue leaves no space for such a possibility as I have been describing. This must raise questions.

In the evening of the same Sunday I went with friends to the church where they normally worship. I have been to the church a number of times and am very familiar with the type of church. It's a good evangelical church with a long history of fidelity to the Gospel. The building was full with a good-sized congregation. A well-known visiting preacher gave us a lengthy exposition from Scripture on the doctrine of Justification by Faith. It was very sound and well argued. But I also found it a bit smug. I got the feeling the preacher was more keen to demonstrate his soundness on the subject than lead the unconverted to an experience of faith. I am sure the congregation was made up of good Christian people, who really loved God and sought to serve him. But there was something lacking; the vibe, the reality, I'd experienced that morning.

As I sat there, not really enjoying what was happening, finding it heavy and dull, I asked myself the question "Where would Jesus have felt more at home today, in this service or the one I attended this morning ?" There was little doubt in my mind as to the answer.

Long Beach California

Before I left Bournemouth I met with Neil the pastor of the gay church. I was impressed by him. That meeting led to another meeting, with the pastor of the MCC church in south London. She had been a missionary in south-east Asia with a large, very well-known, evangelical missionary society. That is, until it was discovered she was a Lesbian. She told me stories of evangelical ministers and leaders with whom she had contact, who were gay but closeted. Some of them visited her church from time to time. One or two were quite well known.

The chain of events continued, the doors kept opening. She told me of an ex-Pentecostal minister who pastored a gay church in Hartford, Connecticut, where I 'happened' to be going the following week. He, on his part, told me of a church in Long Beach, California, not far from my destination of Anaheim, which he said I would love. He gave me the phone number of the pastor, a Dr. Dusty Pruett.

When I got to Anaheim I rang, only to be told that the pastor was in Washington D.C. meeting with President Clinton, to discuss the controversial issue of gays in the military. Dr. Pruett had been an officer in the army and she had been discharged for being gay. After seeing the President, I was told, she was going to Phoenix, Arizona, for a conference. So she would not be available that week. "That's it, God, this door isn't going to open" was my immediate response.

I was just about to put the phone down when the woman on line said "Hold on a minute, are you the person from South Africa?" She couldn't have known that from my very British accent. She went on to say that Dr. Dusty had said, that if a man from South Africa phoned, she was to say that there would be a half-hour slot Friday morning when Dusty would be passing through Long Beach and available. Friday was my last day in southern California.

When I arrived at the agreed time there was no Dusty. Half an hour later, still no Dusty. I walked around the block telling the Lord that I'd give it a few more minutes, but after that I would regard the door as closed. As I was getting ready to leave a plump, rather-motherly, middle-aged woman, rushed into the building and was about to rush out again when she noticed me. She'd forgotten about the appointment, had started out on her journey to Phoenix, but had to return to pick up something she had left behind.

There was only a few minutes in which to tell her the gist of my story. But it only needed that to get her excited. She told me of a prophecy, she had received through a senior pastor friend that God was going to send a man to help her in the work she was doing. She told me that she believed I was that man and asked me to go away and pray about joining her. I had said nothing about looking for a job. It wasn't in my thinking at that stage. I was exploring the scene. But when I got outside the church building I looked up to heaven and said, "Lord I think something significant just happened".

Again, I am aware that this kind of guidance can be suspect.

40

So I was determined to make no rash assumptions or decisions. I continued my trip visiting other gay churches in San Francisco and Vancouver. I was not impressed with either of them. I doubted whether either of the preachers I heard were born again Christians. I felt I couldn't possibly work in these situations, though I would have loved to live in either of those two beautiful cities, both long time favourites of mine.

It put a big doubt into my mind as to whether God really was leading me in the direction of working with a gay church. I was really scared even at the thought. But even as I sat in my hotel room, feeling confused, the Lord spoke to me again. If I wasn't going to do anything about churches like these, how were people in them going to hear the Gospel? And what about the much larger gay community, most of whom didn't know their right hand from their left spiritually?

Time to Decide

I arrived back in South Africa feeling the door was still open, but that I would need a lot more confirmation from God if I was to act. I had six months before I would need to make a final decision. This was the time for praying and praying hard. Day after day I gave myself to serious prayer, calling on God to guard me from any wrong decision, telling him that it was my heart's desire to please him above all else. As the time for decision got nearer, news from Long Beach confirmed the door was open at that end. I began to get really scared.

Then I saw the possibility of a way out. A party of Vineyard pastors came over from California to speak at a conference, held just outside Cape Town. At that time I was working as a pastor, in association with the Vineyard movement. I loved being with these California guys, their laid-back style combined with a warm, open, spirituality. At the conference was a close friend, who knew nothing of my plans, but had been concerned about my future. He was an elder of my church and knew I had committed myself to resigning from my post soon. He also knew I had no new job lined up.

During the conference he asked me about the situation and what I would like to do if I got the chance. I talked about the California guys and how much I would enjoy working with men like these. Typical of my friend, and his genuine concern for me, he got to work quickly trying to pull the right strings. With some pushing from him, the local leader of the Vineyard work contacted the Californian leadership. But I heard nothing, and as the time for decision drew near, I knew God had got me in a corner and that he really did want me to go to Long Beach.

There was one more bit of this story that I didn't hear about for several months. I had moved to the US and was undergoing a barrage of criticism from the wider circle of friends and colleagues who now knew what I was doing. I had waited three months after my arrival before letting them know. I needed some time to be sure I was going to be able to cope.

Some of them questioned the validity of my guidance process because I had omitted to consult with close friends. I acknowledged the truth of that. Consulting with mature friends and colleagues, who know us well, is a key part of the guidance process. But in this case I had known what the answer would be. They would have urged me not to go to California. Most of them would have found it impossible to understand the situation as I saw it from my side of the fence. Most of them suffered from the same kind of blindness, on this issue, that had caused me to live in fear for years.

But it did concern me that I had not checked things out with any evangelical leader, outside the gay scene, who knew me well and whose opinion I valued. I was still ready to receive that counsel, and be rebuked if necessary, by any brother who really loved me and was willing to listen to my story. There was one man in California who could fulfil that role, Dave Owen. He was a South African who knew me quite well, who I respected very much, and who was pastoring a large Vineyard church in Malibu. I visited him, told him my story, and he gave me his blessing. He recognised me as a man whose desire was to follow God and please God. Many of my friends seemed to have decided I was already backslidden. Stories had even spread that I had apostasised; that is, left the true Church. He believed that my guidance story was a solid one. He believed that I really had heard God speak.

He then added a further piece of evidence to support the guidance process. When the Vineyard leaders in Cape Town had contacted the California leadership, Bob Fulton the brother-in-law of John Wimber, and the man responsible for Vineyard work in Africa, had organised a meeting with Dave Owen to discuss how they might use me in the work. The meeting never took place. The biggest earthquake in many years, in Southern California, took place that day in January 1994. The meeting was abandoned and never re-scheduled. But neither of them knew that I had entered the U.S. through another door two months later. Coincidence? OK, but it makes you think doesn't it?

But why did I take that door? Why didn't I try and push the Vineyard one? Why didn't I seek some other door that would have given me access to the gay community?

This was the greatest objection of my friends. They could have accepted me becoming a missionary to gay people. But they regarded it as an unacceptable compromise that I would enter into church fellowship with people who were practising homosexuals, and receive financial support from them. I accept that as valid criticism from their point of view.

Today, I still live with the consequences of it. A dozen years afterwards there are still churches, which I planted, that refuse to ask me to preach. That's in spite of the fact that for the last eleven years I have been pastoring, or working with, regular evangelical churches. The question they asked of me, like many others I get asked, are not easily answered. In the end the only answer I can give is that I believed, and still believe, that God led me in that direction, and that he did it in such a convincing way that I was left with no serious doubt that I had heard him correctly. I would have been disobeying God if I had not gone.

But there is a secondary reason. I do not believe I would have got into the heart of the gay community if I had done it any other way. I believe we need to 'sit where they sit' (as Ezekiel did with the Jews in exile) to understand their plight and their pain. There are orthodox evangelical churches which make a serious attempt to reach gay people. The Vineyard churches are amongst them. But in my experience they only touch the edge of the gay community, people who are already Christians or at least churched, who are unhappy with who they are.

The hard core of gay people is alienated from the Church, particularly evangelical churches. Many of them regard Christians as their chief enemy. They have suffered too much from the extremes of fundamentalist opposition, and even hatred, and so are not open to hear the voice and message of authentic Christianity. I might have tried some other alternative, by starting a new ministry that avoided both the tarnishing of evangelicals and the compromise of gay churches, but it would have been a very long process. Realistically it was too late in life for me to do that. I was prepared to pay the price of the misunderstanding and rejection in order to 'sit where they sit'.

Life in California

My years in California were not easy. I had to take a huge cultural leap at an age when change doesn't come so easily. Standing my ground theologically wasn't easy. For most gay people the terms evangelical and fundamentalist mean the same thing. It didn't take me long to understand why there is so much enmity towards conservative Christians. Many of the folk in the church came from that background and had not been well treated.

At Gay Pride parades there were always fundamentalist groups in evidence, standing by the roadside, with hateful banners and sometimes screaming religious obscenities. At the same time there were more liberal church groups marching in the parades in support of gay rights. It helped to underline the belief that it is evangelicals who are the enemy. But the liberal churches, who appeared to be friends, usually had no Gospel. Their message could be summed up "Don't worry, God loves you anyway." There was no emphasis on the need to know personal salvation through Christ, straight and gay alike. It made my position difficult.

One Sunday morning I arrived at church to find a group of fundamentalist extremists standing across the road with the usual banners, and shouting crude denunciations. As I came around the corner one shouted, "Here comes another of the faggots." I walked across the road, offered him my hand, and introduced myself as a born-again Christian who had been serving God in Africa as a missionary for more than 25 years. It threw him off his stride for a moment and he was about to take my hand when another member of the group yelled, "Don't touch him, you might get AIDS!"

I told him how I thought God saw what they were doing. "I don't know what you imagine is taking place in that church building right now," I said, "but I believe that what you are doing is more sinful in the eyes of God than anything you are imagining." The leader replied that he'd never sinned in his life! The group probably related to an Independent Baptist pastor, the Revd. Fred Phelps, who is well known for taking groups of protesters to funerals of AIDS victims, particularly well known ones. They usually carry banners announcing that the deceased is already burning in hell.

By the time I got into the church service worship was well underway. There was a joy and vibrancy about it that morning. Having just come through the gauntlet the folk were rejoicing that God loved them, even if there were so-called Christians out there who hated them. I asked Dusty if I could say a few words. I reminded them of my commitment to an evangelical view of the Gospel, but went on to make very clear that what they had just experienced had nothing to do with evangelical Christianity or any form of true Christianity. These men were not Christians at all, whatever they professed.

But it was hard for many of the folk to distinguish, because so many had been hurt by churches. For a while I led a house group for Bible study and prayer. Two particular women in the group, who were in a relationship, impressed me. One of them, Linda, had such knowledge of the Bible and the ways of God, that I realised she came from a strong Christian background. Her partner was a woman she had led to the Lord. Linda had been a worship leader in a well-known Charismatic church. She had been put out of the church when it was discovered she was in a Lesbian relationship.

I understand why churches feel they have to do that sometimes. It's the way that it is done which is the real sin. Her family were also members of the same church and they rejected her too, making her feel she had no part in the Kingdom of God. She had taken to drink and for a while had a serious alcohol problem. But her genuine faith and desire for God brought her to the Long Beach church.

I was in my office one day when she arrived in a state of considerable distress. Her sister had recently had a baby, Linda's first niece. Linda and her partner were about to move to Florida. They felt called to serve God there. She wanted to see her niece before making the several thousand mile move. But her sister had refused, saying that she didn't want her child to be contaminated by a Lesbian. Linda was so upset that she'd gone straight to the nearest bar. Only as she had the glass in her hand did she decide to come to the church for prayer, instead of trying to drown her sorrows. All she had gone through was done in the name of evangelical Christianity.

It wasn't easy preaching. The congregations of gay churches, even ones where the pastors have an evangelical background and believe in the new birth, often get a mixed diet of Biblical religion and gay politics. There were obviously limitations in what I could preach.

I was still re-thinking my own beliefs as to what the Bible taught about homosexuality, and how that could be reconciled with contemporary thinking on the causes of homosexuality. I was also trying to find where the line had to be drawn between folk who were struggling to be faithful and monogamous, and those who were just set on a life of promiscuous enjoyment. I had to be faithful without closing the ears of my hearers, or losing opportunities to preach. I needed to prove that I cared about them and their struggles, needs, and disappointments, because I shared their problems.

In every new pastorate I've commenced I've had to tread carefully at first, in order to win my listeners before I could begin to correct them. With the Long Beach congregation I was convinced that if I could draw them closer to Christ, by exalting him, the work of the Holy Spirit within them would begin to bring about change. I saw that begin to happen. I saw a few folk converted. I saw others growing in their faith and commitment.

I saw a few leave the church and return to main-stream evangelical churches because they had become strong enough to do that. One young man, who had been involved in worship leading, was convicted by the Holy Spirit while he was leading his band during a Gay Pride Festival rave. He felt that too much of what was going on around him was not compatible with his developing relationship to Christ. He left the platform in the middle of the dance session and soon after returned to the Vineyard church where he had once worshipped. I had noted over a period of time the intensity with which he had been listening to my preaching.

Living with AIDS

It wasn't easy ministering to folk who had developed AIDS. My time there was before anti-retroviral drugs were introduced.

People were dying all the time, including people in the congregation, most of them young men. The loss and pain had devastated many in the church. One of my colleagues on the staff had to take a very early retirement as his health deteriorated.

My first weekend in Long Beach, during the evening service, I was approached by a lady to ask if I would go with her, and pray for a young man dying in a nearby hospice. He was in his early twenties, nothing but skin and bone, obviously near the end. He lay on his bed in his room. I'd never faced anything like this. I knew from the beginning of my time there that I must not hesitate to touch and embrace those sick with AIDS. The fear of touching is irrational, because it's almost impossible to become infected that way, unless blood and open cuts are involved. But the fear is enough to cause hesitation. Gay people suffering with AIDS look for hesitation and read you through it.

So immediately I took him in my arms, talked to him of Jesus and prayed with him. He died a couple of days later. From that time onwards I never hesitated to take the initiative in ministering to the dying. The gay community was so weary of death that some on staff tended to avoid it. But for me it was one of the most meaningful things I did. It brought reality to my words. Some of the young men I visited regularly, to bring comfort and support, died and some I had to bury. They had become my friends by then.

Jaime, a young Mexican-American with a Mormon background, came to Christ during that period. The last time I saw him in church he'd been asked to help in serving communion for the first time. I remember the smile on his face as he savoured the enjoyment of this privilege. Preaching at his funeral was not only very meaningful, as I declared the power of the risen Christ to raise him, with a renewed body, on the Last Day. It was also meaningful because of the many folk at the funeral from his own family, and the family of his partner, folk from evangelical backgrounds and the very conservative Mormons. Some came very reluctantly to a service led by a pastor of a gay church. The evangelicals were amazed to hear the Biblical Gospel so clearly preached. His partner of several years, John, needed my support for the rest of my time in that church. I kept contact with him afterwards. His grieving was as intense as any heterosexual person who loses his partner. This is something which straight people seem to find difficult to understand.

Another young man who I befriended was Steve. He was already seriously sick when I arrived. He would rally for a while and then sickness would strike again, leaving him weaker each time. Like many of these guys he had been wild in his teens. A typical blond gay beauty before his illness, he had worked as a prostitute. I realised that his active days were nearly over and offered to take him on a trip, anywhere he wanted to go. He named Palm Springs in the desert. It was only when we got there that he told me that he was well-known in this small town. It was the town where he had plied his trade! He dragged me round jewellery shops and clothes shops, acutely embarrassing me by calling out several times, so all the world could hear, "Reverend come and look at this." On the trip I talked about facing death. He said something I've never forgotten. "I don't so much mind about dying," he said, "as I care about the fact that no one will remember me within a short time of my death." He had been brought up in an orphanage, and was later sexually abused by a foster father. There were few in the world who would be affected by his passing.

Time to Move on?

I was at Long Beach less than two years. Local church politics determined my future. Dr. Dusty was fired because the church board felt she had got the church into serious debt. The church had a policy that in the event of the senior pastor standing down, for whatever reason, the rest of the staff had to stand down as well.

I could have applied for the job of senior pastor myself, but that would have put me into a position where I might be faced with compromises my conscience wouldn't allow. I could have tried to move to another church, but my work visa only allowed me to work with this church. So with only a brief period of notice I was without a job and not allowed to stay in the USA. I took this to be God's closure. The door he had opened he had now closed.

My work as a missionary to the gay community hadn't lasted long and it seemed that I had not achieved a great deal. But I learned so much in those two years about myself, about gay people, and so much of it was positive and has enabled me to speak with knowledge and authority about this rejected community. What did I learn?

I learned that suffering brings people closer together. The AIDS epidemic devastated the Gay community. Since that time the devastation has moved to Africa; where it has become a problem of horrendous proportions. But it was the Gay community that took the first brunt, and possibly the proportion of Gay men who died in that period was higher even than the percentage of deaths in African countries today. So many folk saw their partners die knowing that it was only a matter of time before they followed. Sometimes they had lost more than one partner and often they had lost many friends as well.

It wouldn't be an exaggeration to say it was a community in a state of shock. That had created its own instability, to add to the instability already existing in the Gay community. Randy Shilt's book, made into a film, "And the band played on" traces the story graphically. But out of that pain grew a great deal of love and sacrifice.

I will never forget the annual memorial services on International Aids Day. There was a part of the service when people were given the opportunity to call out the names of loved-ones and friends who had died that year. There was the great AIDS quilt being created in sections, in many different parts of America and further afield, each section having an individual tribute to someone who had died. Usually a sizeable piece, maybe filling a whole church wall, would be on display at these services.

There were moments in these gatherings when a collective sense of emotion touched feelings so deep that it was overwhelming. A sigh, barely audible, but very powerful would rise up as if it came from one heart. I've rarely experienced anything like it. It made me glad to be there and to feel the pain of this community. It happens to nations in times of war and other disasters, but is normally short lived. Gay people have gone through so much down the centuries that it has given a sense of togetherness which I have missed in the years since I left Long Beach. My involvement is now only occasional. But the impact of those two years will last till the day I die.

People on the Fringes: Transgendered

I learned about people who were much more on the fringes of society than me; people I hardly ever had contact with in my safe evangelical church background.

People like Mary-Anne. I saw her my first Sunday morning in the Long Beach church. I had noticed that almost all the women wore trousers, not so commonplace then as it is now. I was looking around to see if any Lesbians wore really feminine clothes. I saw a skirt but it took only a moment to realise this was a man wearing an atrociously made wig and an ill-fitting women's outfit. When we were introduced I found it very difficult to address him/her as Mary-Anne. I realised I was going through the same feelings as many people have to homosexuals like me. I never got to know her story. I don't think she was gay or even a transgendered person. She didn't fit in any particular category. But this was what she wanted, and felt she needed, to be. Why else would anyone bring so much ridicule on herself as she must have experienced? A gay church was about the only place she would find acceptance.

Later on I had to get involved in a much more complicated situation. One Sunday evening, while I was preaching, I noticed a well-dressed middle-aged man with longish hair, sitting in the congregation. I hadn't seen him before and I couldn't help noticing him because he was crying. By the time I'd finished he was sobbing so much that I found it difficult to make much sense of what he said to me. I invited him to come and see me during the week. He was a visitor from Pennsylvania who had come to Long Beach to try and discover more about himself. He planned to drive up to San Francisco the next day but agreed to visit me on his return. About an hour before the appointment he rang to say he was in a traffic jam and would be late.

When he finally arrived, and rang the bell, I opened the door and for a second thought I had another caller. But in the same split second I realised that it was the right person, but dressed as a smart middle-aged lady. He was very embarrassed. He had intended going to his hotel to change before coming to me, but because of his lateness felt it was unfair to keep me waiting longer. He began to apologise but I had the sense to cut him off and say that no apology was needed; I was quite accustomed to the situation. It wasn't true, but I felt I had to do something quickly, to prevent further distress of the kind I'd experienced with him on the Sunday.

The reality was that my mind was reeling as to what kind of story I was about to hear, and more importantly, how was I going to deal with it. He was a businessman from a small conservative town. He had a fairly important position with a well-known department store chain. He had been married for more than twenty years. He was an elder of an evangelical church. Throughout the years of his marriage he had known there was something wrong. Part of him felt he wanted to be a woman; that he was in fact a woman trapped in a man's body. The furthest he'd gone, in trying to express it, was by sometimes wearing ladies underwear. A few years before, his wife had found the underwear tucked at the bottom of a drawer, but said nothing. So he'd assumed she was coping with his problem.

The time came when he decided to tell her the truth. She wasn't prepared at all, freaked out so badly, that he twice tried suicide and had to be hospitalised. Prior to discharge from a psychiatric unit he had been counselled to take time off, go away, and try and discover who he wanted to be. Hence his trip to California, a place where he was more likely to find people like himself, and acceptance for a different lifestyle. I realised that he had been to San Francisco as part of that search. I asked him about the trip. He'd visited the various bars dressed as a woman. When I asked whether he'd had sexual contact with anyone he confessed he'd had a 'fumble' in the bushes with a man he'd met at a rest-stop en route. It hadn't gone beyond a kiss and cuddle but as he described it I saw, for the first time, a small smile. "It was wonderful" he said.

What was I to say to him? He had already tried suicide twice. I painted the picture of what would probably happen if he pursued this direction. He would need to move to somewhere like LA. He would never find acceptance in the town from which he came. That would mean leaving his job, his church and almost certainly his wife. He was horrified. He didn't want to lose any of these. He really did love his wife in his own way. I pointed out that this only left one acceptable way ahead. He would need to seek God's grace and help to pick up the pieces of the life he had lived for more than twenty years, as best he could. He couldn't have it both ways. He looked very sad. I was very gentle with him. I counselled him further and prayed with him, and asked him to let me know how he got on when he returned home.

I never heard from him again. I've often wondered about him. I did what I felt I had to do but felt too that I'd failed him. I'd never been equipped for dealing with people like him. Society in general is becoming much more compassionate with people like him, but it is my experience that evangelical Christians are not. He doesn't fit into any of our categories of how people should act. In many evangelical churches he would still be treated as someone perverse and perverted. But why would a respectable middle-aged man, an elder of a church, who had lived his life as a Christian man, want to be as a woman if there was not something very deep inside him that cried out for fulfilment? No one invites that amount of ridicule and rejection unless they see no alternative.

During the last two years I have twice been invited to meet with the elders of a large evangelical church to share my story. They had received an application for membership from a transgendered person. He was a married man and a born-again Christian. He and his wife had separated. After lengthy counselling he had undergone surgery and was now living as a woman. Many months later the elders had still not decided what they should do, even though they were in no doubt that he/she was a true Christian, and he was already involved in the life of their church. I don't minimise their difficulty. But my time in Long Beach has enabled me to relate better to the real world.

Many evangelicals have a serious problem, which will increasingly bring scorn on us from the world, because we are seen as a people who lack compassion. We have determined that there are only two categories of people sexually and psychologically. There is no room in our theology for there being variation even though we say we believe in the Fall.

People on the Fringes: Paedophiles

I think too of John, who joined the Long Beach church while I was there. He was a quiet kindly young man, who played the organ from time to time for Sunday services. He became part of a circle of friends I hung around with. It was only after I left that I discovered that he had served a period in prison for paedophile acts.

There is great public concern about this crime at the present time. Many people's attitudes towards perpetrators is 'lock 'em up and throw away the key'. There has been such agitation in some parts of England, when paedophiles have completed their sentence and been released to go back into society, that on one occasion serious damage was done to the man's house - except they'd got the wrong house! There is no question it is a very serious crime, but this kind of hateful hysteria is itself evil.

Getting to know John, before knowing about his crime, made me realise that perpetrators are real people too with needs. At that point in his life what John needed above all was acceptance and love. He didn't attempt to justify what he had done. But he was also another victim of the abnormalities that a fallen world sometimes throws up. He was not gay, and subsequently married a woman in the church who had teenage boys by a previous marriage. I knew the woman well and had great respect for her as a serious Christian. Her boys were young teenagers but they came, with their mother, to my Bible studies and responded in an amazingly mature and spiritual way to the teaching. What news I have received over the years suggests that the marriage has worked well. But John could so easily have fallen between the cracks in society. He came to a gay church because it was the only place where people were likely to show acceptance. It's the hurting who are most likely to understand and help others who hurt. I am profoundly grateful for that period amongst people like that.

Good Times and Bad Times

I also learned to have fun in a new way because, for the first time, I could express something I'd always had inside me-what's often called 'camp'. I certainly dressed up in my mother's clothes and sister's clothes as a child, but you don't do that as a straight adult unless you are very confident of your male image. I hated it when I was forced into cross-dressing sometimes at church concerts, because I wasn't confident of my image. Now I could relax when I was with folk like me, and get something out of my system, though I still avoided cross-dressing.

There are, of course, many jokes about gay men having a strong feminine side and lesbians a strong masculine side. On one occasion I visited a gay church in Pretoria to which I've referred earlier. The pastor had previously been an ordained minister of the very conservative Dutch Reformed Church. The congregation he had planted for gay people was named "The Reforming Church", and in its worship, the use of the Afrikaans language, and its general organisation, it was modelled on the DRC. The church was predominantly male. Like many churches they decided to raise funds by having a cake sale at the local shopping mall on a Saturday morning.

Gay men are noted for being good cooks, so there was no difficulty in presenting an impressive display of cakes and other confectionery. The stall was entirely staffed by younger men much to the surprise of the local Afrikaaner ladies, out to do their shopping. "Where are your wives?" was a frequent question. "Oh, they're at home watching the rugby on TV", the reply. Rugby is the second religion of the Afrikaans-speaking community, and Saturday the day when the typically macho Afrikaans men are glued to the TV, beer in one hand, a boerwors roll in the other. In the gay community I don't have to pretend to be macho. There is a side of me that can find expression that I had long had to repress to keep up my image. But it gave me the confidence to become more fully myself in the whole of life.

There were a whole lot of other things I learned that I'll leave for other chapters. But in that brief period of my life I learned more, perhaps, than at any other period, and I made some very good friends as well.

My dismissal from the church left me with a very serious financial problem. I had put almost all my capital into the purchase of a one-bedroom condominium by the beach. It had become my haven where I could withdraw when things were difficult. I loved it and still sometimes miss it. As soon as I got home from the office out would come my bike, and I'd be away down the beach path with many other cyclists, joggers and folk on roller-blades. Unfortunately the market had slumped since I bought the property and all attempts to sell failed, even at a considerably reduced price. I was into negative equity, the mortgage owner's nightmare. The realtors advised me to hand in the keys and write it off. I attempted to find a tenant but I couldn't get enough rent to cover the mortgage.

I was rescued by two of the friends I used to hang out with, a gay couple, who offered to take responsibility for it after I had left. For more than two years they looked after it, found tenants, and made up the difference between the rent and the mortgage. Only when the market had improved did they sell it, so that I recovered a sizeable part of the capital I had invested. The flat I've been living in until recently, in Cape Town, was bought with the money they rescued. They have remained very good friends.

Back to England

Forced to leave America I took the only route that seemed open to me, return to my homeland of England, where I had not lived for nearly thirty years.

It was too early to return to South Africa and would have been too painful. More importantly, I was unlikely to find work. I had remained celibate and in theory celibacy is the only requirement for a gay man exercising ministry, in any of the main-line denominations. But the practice is sometimes different.

Homophobia is still alive and well in evangelical church life. My involvement in the gay community had blackened my reputation, even though I had been responding to a missionary call from God. A colleague, who I had worked with in Cape Town immediately before leaving for America, had preached a sermon in which he suggested that my real motivation for going to the US was otherwise. He suggested I was looking for a partner. The tape of the sermon was distributed quite widely. When I returned to South Africa for a visit, soon after my return to England, a formal meeting was arranged at which I asked him for an apology. He refused to give it.

So England seemed to be the only place to go. I had approached the Baptist Union some three years before, with a view to resuming the ministry I had with them after leaving Spurgeon's College in 1963. I renewed contact. But it was the recommendation of a minister friend, who knew my story in full, that led to me becoming pastor of a large Baptist Church in Reading, west of London. In the application process I was open about the kind of ministry I had been exercising in California. I even gave them a letter of recommendation from the Long Beach church.

But they asked me no direct questions about my sexual orientation. I think both sides were operating on a "Don't ask, don't tell" policy. The majority of them thought I was the right man for the job and so didn't want to ask a question that would have messed things up. It was an evangelical church but not fundamentalist. I found the leaders were compassionate people in handling one or two openly gay people in the congregation. I was able to become involved locally in the Buddies programme, which seeks to help HIV+ people who have developed full blown AIDS. I was on the committee and nearly all of those involved were gay, but this raised no questions from the church.

As my work amongst gay people became known, various groups in my church asked me to speak on the subject, as did one or two other churches. It was a time when many Christians were reading Philip Yancey's book, *"What's so amazing about Grace?"* Whilst maintaining a traditional evangelical understanding of what the Bible says about homosexuality, Yancey pleads for a much more compassionate and embracing approach from churches. He refers to Mel White, a close friend of his, whose experience had profoundly shaken him.

This book led the leaders of one largish Baptist church in the town to reconsider their policy. I was asked to speak at an evening service on the subject, and answer questions. I still thought it unwise to declare my own orientation. But gay folk in the congregation worked me out and talked privately. In spite of my assurances that the leadership was open to change, they were still afraid to come out of the closet. One referred to the fact that the pastor had mimicked gay people from the pulpit not long before. I told the leaders that they would need to do a lot more than they realised, to get gay people to trust them. One of the men I talked with had been put out of an evangelical church in another town, and did not want to risk the trauma of that happening again.

Out of the Closet

Near the end of my four years in Reading an incident arose which forced me out of the closet. The Labour Government of Tony Blair was proposing to abolish a piece of anti-gay legislation, Section 28 as it was called, implemented by Margaret Thatcher. It put certain strictures on school teachers as to what they could teach about homosexuality in class. When in it fact it was removed from the statute book, about two years later, the decision got all-party support.

But in 2000 it was still seen, by a lot of evangelical Christians, as promoting family values. I was part of a ministers' group that embraced the majority of evangelical ministers in the town. I was also part of the leadership committee. During my absence, through sickness, a small group within the fraternal drew up a letter strongly condemning what the government was about to do. It was to be sent to the local members of Parliament and to the press. Almost forty ministers signed it, probably ninety per cent of evangelical ministers in the town. By the time I got to see it the die was already cast.

I was horrified, horrified by lack of understanding of the issues, horrified by the bad arguments, and horrified by the thought of what it would do to gay Christians in the town, and gay people in general. I contacted the leadership immediately and urged them to re-think. I also told them, for the first time, of my sexual orientation. They were extremely sympathetic but felt they had to abide by the decision and send the letter. But they also agreed with me that it was right that I should send a letter of my own, to the press and the MPs, expressing my dissent. I warned them that it would all get blown up beyond their expectations, and be far-reaching in its effects.

I was right. Their letter, intended for the 'letters to the editor' section of the local newspaper, became the front page article with a sensational banner headline. I kept back my letter until the following week. In what I wrote I tried to minimise the force of what would happen. I expressed my warm appreciation for my ministerial brothers and my respect for their efforts in the town. I stressed that my disagreement with them was on this one issue. But I expressed my concern for the effect their letter would have on gay people who already felt rejected by the church.

Days before my letter was published one of the two Reading members of Parliament called me, and then a reporter from the rival local newspaper. His interview led to an equally sensational heading - pointing out not only my disagreement with so many fellow-ministers, but the two other pastors of my own church! The correspondence in the press continued for many weeks, far exceeding any other response the newspapers had ever had. I was described, in some of the letters, as 'a typical liberal with relativist views of morality'. Others attacked me as having no understanding of family life or parenthood, because I was unmarried.

In general, evangelical Christians were critical of me, non-Christians were supportive of me. As so often happens, when we get involved with the press, Christians did not acquit themselves well. Their arguments came over as weak and based more on bigotry than reason. I got two or three angry phone calls from ministers berating me, and expressing shock that I was not the man of God they had thought me to be.

But the tide began to flow my way. I was contacted by youth pastors and workers, from evangelical churches, thanking me for being willing to stick out my neck. They said they were embarrassed by the tone of the letter signed by their senior pastors. They described the reality they faced working with young people. They were frequently dealing with young people struggling with their sexuality, and hurt by the apparent rejection of church leaders. But heterosexual young people were also critical of the attitudes of their leaders. Many of them had friends who were gay, and were decent, caring people, not the perverts or monsters that traditional evangelical thinking had often portrayed them as being.

A member of my own congregation, who was a professor in the University, thanked me for my courage. He said that as someone who was day after day working with students, he had found it very hard trying to defend traditional evangelical attitudes to gay people. The world outside the church had changed considerably but Christians were ill-prepared to deal with these changes.

Some weeks later, when my time for leaving my church and the country was near, the same ministers' group put on a farewell lunch for me, to which about half of them came. They presented me with a bound book which contained their individual tributes to me and my ministry. They also asked me if I would be willing to address them on the subject of homosexuality. I shared my own story and urged them to reconsider their approach to gay people. I spoke of the necessity of thinking through how the church handles its relationship to society and the State. Their letter had come over as arrogant, telling people who for the most part were not Christians or believers in God, nor in the Bible, how to govern their own lives. The Church in England has so often made the mistake of preaching morality to society instead of the Good News.

At the end of my talk several admitted they had made a serious mistake in sending the letter. One of the key leaders in the group said, "Graham, how are we going to manage without you around to give us insight on these issues?" Several said, "Graham, we respect you more not less for what you have told us about yourself". So I left the town encouraged to believe there is a change taking place amongst Christian leaders; though I was not fooled into thinking that these men represented the thinking of all their colleagues. During the weeks that followed I was contacted by gay Christians in the town, people I didn't know, saying how much it had meant to them that someone like me had been prepared to speak up on their behalf. That in particular made it worth it all.

Back to South Africa

The time had come for my return to South Africa. I wanted to go back and pick up where I'd left off some years before, fulfilling God's call to serve African young people. God had spoken to me while in Reading, through circumstances and through the urging of the Holy Spirit, to go to Port Elizabeth and work amongst black University students. Friends in Britain and America offered to support me to do this work. They are still supporting me.

I have never been lacking in very good and faithful friends who stand by me in all circumstances. Some of them had worked with me in Zambia and knew the value of impacting the student community for Christ. Their belief in me was to prove very important. I discovered there were still those in South Africa prepared to write me off, and say I was unfit for Christian ministry.

I worked with a particular church in Port Elizabeth which had a large number of students. But I was not on the staff or supported financially by them. I told the pastor my story and, with one or two assurances from me, he was happy to accept me as a co-worker. I spent four very wonderful, very rewarding years there; but had very little contact with the local gay community.

One particular incident, however, confirmed that every local church is faced with the issue of how to minister to gay people.

It involved a young professional white man in his early thirties, who frequently led worship in this large congregation. He was one of the best worship leaders I have ever come across. His joy in Christ and enthusiasm to worship could ignite the whole congregation. He was loved and respected by the people. Few could have been aware that he had struggled from early years with the fact that he was gay.

Then he fell in love. I came back from leave in Cape Town to be told by the pastor that he had left the church. He asked for my help. With some difficulty I contacted him and spent a brief time with him. From then on, however, he appeared to avoid further contact with me or the church. For years this young man had coped with his problem because of the strength of his relationship to Christ. Until one day 'Mr Right' came along and romantic love changed his perspective, at least at that moment. In the brief period I was with him it was very obvious that he was head over heels in love. He looked different. He was dressed differently. All the same symptoms as when a heterosexual person gets the 'love bug'. The process is the same, the feelings the same and the blindness that frequently accompanies it is the same. I knew that he would not come back to that church in the near future. He wanted nothing to spoil this wonderful new thing that had happened in his life. He knew the leaders would not understand and would not know how to handle it. I was sad that he did not trust me either. In spite of all I said to him, about my own experience, I represented also an organisation that had no real place for people like him.

Return to Cape Town

The time came, when I completed the circle, and returned 'home', to Cape Town. The question of which church I would join came to the forefront. I needed somewhere where I would be accepted and given opportunities to minister.

I have pastored three churches in Cape Town and been

involved in planting two or three others. Most of the men now leading those churches are men I have pastored and helped train and equip for ministry. A group of churches now exists in South Africa which developed out of what I planted.   But with one exception it soon became clear they all felt that I was 'not kosher' for ministry.

It was the twentieth anniversary of when I planted the mother church of this group. Most people assumed I would be asked to participate in the special celebrations, to which many folk had been invited. But it was made clear by the pastor (who had got his job through me) and the elders (men I had pastored) that I would only be invited if I was prepared to be 'interrogated' first. I was told that there were some 'serious issues' they wanted to raise. I refused to meet with them in those circumstances, but offered to meet informally with one or two and let them ask their questions. I had what I thought was a frank but very friendly meeting with the pastor.

I thought we had laid an excellent foundation for future contact. But shortly afterward stories spread that it had not gone well and I was still 'unacceptable'. I had let it be known that I would be working with a Baptist Church, the pastor of which was an old friend, who knew my whole story and accepted me unconditionally. But one day he got a phone call from one of those elders urging him not to use me in ministry.

That hit me hard. All these men had been blessed and nurtured by me, but they were willing to try and block my ministry not just from their group of churches, but throughout the city, and in doing so rob me of my livelihood. I'd passed retirement age but I still needed to work and earn. And they knew there was no evidence that I had ever had sex. There isn't any. I have been celibate. But it is enough for them that I have stood up and spoken up for the gay community and the injustices against that community.

The evangelical scene is very mixed at the moment. There are men, like John, the pastor of the Baptist Church that welcomed me. Men like some of those in Reading. But there are others for whom homophobia is still very much a driving force. And I know some of the people who they have hurt and are still hurting. I find myself still counselling them from time to time.

Chapter Three - Why is it so difficult for Evangelical Christians to accept change ?

Changes in Society

Society in the western world is rapidly changing its attitude toward homosexuality. That is an undeniable fact. The European Parliament, which will soon represent almost thirty nations, has made it increasingly difficult for any member state to maintain laws that discriminate in any way against homosexuals. Britain has had to change some of its legislation because of that.

It is now taken for granted that homosexual orientation comes from nature not nurture. So people in general see it is as wrong to discriminate against homosexuals, in the same way as it is wrong to discriminate against people because of their ethnicity, colour, culture, religion, age or gender. There are well-known people in almost every area of life who are now openly gay. For the most part it no longer works against them.

There have been several prominent members of the British government in recent years who have been openly gay. Michael Portillo, a former Conservative cabinet minister, said a while ago on TV that he thought there might well be a gay Prime Minister in Britain within twenty years. Like it or not there is already one gay Anglican bishop in the USA, and it nearly happened in Britain not so long ago. It will happen, without a shadow of doubt, at some point in the not too distant future.

Let me state now that my purpose in this book is not to justify that kind of action, especially if the person in question is in an actively gay relationship. But the truth is that there have always been gay people in prominent positions, including in the royal family. It has simply not been generally known.

Not Every Change is Right

Of course changes in society are not, in themselves, reasons for Christians, or the church, changing. Sometimes the very opposite. On many issues the church has to hold its ground whatever society says or does. At the present time there is increasing animosity toward the evangelical form of Christianity, because we insist that Christ is the only mediator between man and God. That kind of exclusivity is anathema to post-modern thinking. But that part of our belief is totally non-negotiable. Without it, true Christian religion ceases to exist. We stand for it, we fight for it.

But are traditional views on homosexuality in the same category? Are these views central to the Christian faith and essential for salvation? Of course not. Only a few verses of Scripture even mention the subject. It's not dealt with in the Gospels at all. Can we present a reasonable case, that the common man will understand, as to why we should carry on giving the cold-shoulder to gay people?

I experience the cold-shoulder regularly. Perhaps more importantly, *can we give an explanation, that Christians who are gay can reasonably be expected to understand and accept?* I'm talking about Christians who hold to all the salvation doctrines of the Christian faith, but are treated as morally sick for something they cannot change. For most gay people their sexual orientation is as fixed as the colour of their eyes or their skin.

The theologian may continue to defend his arguments, but they will increasingly appear bigoted and cruel to modern people, including modern Christians. The Gospel has to be preached in the context of the world in which we live. Our arguments in defence of the traditional approach to gay people are beginning to look distinctly threadbare. Why is it so difficult for many evangelical Christians even to take a serious second look at the issue?

Gay Stereotypes

One reason, I think, is because of gay stereotypes. On TV sitcoms gay people are often portrayed as amiable fools; good for a laugh. Some gay men have such a strong feminine side that they are painfully obvious. There are two gay men who regularly sit at the bar at a restaurant where I eat. I just can't help being embarrassed by the way they act. I can see the looks on the face of the barman. Some lesbians look and act like all-in wrestlers. Then, of course, there are the outrageous people we see on TV news after a Gay Pride parade.

But that is a very incomplete picture. It's generally agreed by all the surveys done that about 4% of the population is genuinely gay by orientation. Some put the figure higher, a few slightly lower. But 4% is a reasonable figure to use. That means that in the average smaller church there will be 3 or 4 people who are gay by orientation, just as there will be a certain proportion of people who are left-handed. In a larger church there may be as many as 20 or 30, or even more.

Many folk would think it inconceivable that there are that number of gay people in their church. But that is because they are not for the most part easily recognisable. Most of them may not be sexually active, but that does not change their orientation. The thoughts that wander during a boring sermon, will sometimes be wandering in the direction of someone of the same sex. But otherwise they are more or less the same as anyone else in the congregation, ordinary, hard-working, civilised human beings with the same problems and failures as anyone else.

A few years back I was staying for a while with an older couple who are good friends of mine. I had expected the wife to be very critical after I had come out as being gay. She had some strong opinions on a number of social issues. Then one day she told me what had influenced her thinking. Her daughter-in-law was a nurse who worked with a very fine woman doctor who was a Christian. The doctor was held in great respect by her colleagues, patients and the community in general. She died suddenly. It was only at the funeral that the daughter-in-law discovered that the doctor was a lesbian. The service was in a gay church and her lesbian partner took part in the service. There were many other members of the gay community, as well as many from the straight community, who loved and respected her and paid tribute to her. It is as misleading and wrong to stereotype gay people because of excesses, as it is to stereotype people in your street because some are immoral or dishonest.

Over-Simplification

A second factor that blurs the thinking of evangelicals is the over-simplification of human sexuality.

The world is not as God first created it to be. It doesn't help to keep going back to Genesis 1 and 2 and pointing out that God created only male and female, and nothing in between. That was true then, and true still for the overwhelming majority of people. But there are others caught somewhere in the middle through various effects of the Fall.

The doctrine of the Fall is central to Biblical doctrine, and a core evangelical belief. Why then do we leave it out of the equation when discussing homosexuality ? There are people born with serious deformities which make it even difficult to determine whether they are male or female. There are people with serious psychological deformities which make them feel they are women trapped in a man's body, or men trapped in a woman's body.

There is variation in sexuality amongst people who are in other respects 'normal'. The Bible speaks of people who have the ability to be celibate and those who have not, a variation in sex drive. Paul recommends that in certain situations people remain celibate, even though Genesis 1 and 2 make it clear that marriage is God's purpose for people and procreation is a command of God. Evangelical Christians practice birth control in spite of that command.

There are people who marry but are not able to have children, and therefore not able to fulfil one of the chief purposes of marriage. I will refer later to Kinsey's scale of human sexuality, that suggests that heterosexual men have a feminine side, and vice-versa with women, and that it is stronger in some than in others.

One of the effects of the Fall is that male headship has frequently become perverted to male dominance and male abuse of the female. This is a big issue in our time. In trying to deal with it there is considerable stress on the need for the male to discover his female side. Being macho is no longer seen as a virtue. It is now OK to give a man flowers as a gift. We have a new term in our sexual vocabulary, 'metrosexual', describing the young man about town who is not afraid of revealing the female side of his character.

David Beckham, a modern icon, is a prime example. No one thinks it odd anymore for men to wear jewellery, have fancy hair styles or wear pink shirts. Gay people are another part of this complex picture. No matter how much evangelicals try to explain away homosexuality as being a perversion encouraged by modern culture, and resulting from personal choice, or a result of early nurture, society no longer shares that view. Modern opinion, including medical opinion, believes that some people are born with a homosexual orientation and no amount of effort to change it does change it.

The Claims of the Ex-Gay Movement

This leads to a further factor that creates an un-willingness to re-think, which is the claims of the ex-gay movement. Books and articles are written containing testimonies of people who say they have been 'cured'. What it usually means is that they have been helped to move from being practising homosexuals to non-practising. I have no quarrel with that.

In fact there have been recent signs that this movement is giving up claims that homosexuality can be cured. The American evangelical magazine *"Christianity Today"* has a report in its October 2007 edition of the annual conference of Exodus International the umbrella body which unites various ex-gay groups. A more sober attitude to the possibilities of cure has in part come about because of the number of leaders, as well as many others, who have left the organisation in disillusionment. The emphasis is now more on celibacy than change of sexual orientation.

But I can also offer my own evidence that such changes frequently do not last. I have already referred to a friend whose life-story I know in detail. He has been married for more than twenty years, has children, has been through the courses of the ex-gay movement. He has been a teacher and leader of these courses. He is a strong Christian who desires, with all his heart, not to be attracted to men. For a period of time in quite recent years he thought the physical desire for sex with men had gone. But at the end of the day he is as homosexually oriented as he was in his teens.

Only time tells whether there has been a fundamental change; and with those folk for whom 'cures' are claimed, time usually shows the opposite. People who are not genuinely gay can become involved in homosexual acts as a result of nurture, culturalisation or circumstances. Change of conduct is for them a realistic possibility. But that does not alter the fact that others are stuck with who they are for life. Becoming a Christian does not in itself change that. These people are entitled to be respected and accepted, especially by churches.

Homophobia

A further blockage is simply homophobia. The Oxford dictionary describes it as "a hatred or fear of homosexuals". The fear part is particularly pertinent to what I want to say. It is common these days to begin an anti-gay statement with "I am not homophobic. I love gay people". It was equally common in apartheid South Africa for white people who supported the system to begin with the statement, "I am not a racist. I love black people". If you talk with white people in South Africa today, the great majority claim that they never supported apartheid. It's amazing that it could ever have existed, if one believes people's statements.

The truth is that some of them really do believe what they say, because they were blind to the wrongness of their attitudes at the time. I believe that is true with some Christians, and a lot of non-Christians, when it comes to gay people. The aversion is not so much moral as it is aesthetic, as someone once put it to me. The straight person is repulsed by the thought of sex with someone of the same sex; even being touched inappropriately by such a person. He can't understand therefore why anyone else would want to do it. It has to be perverse and evil. But the aversion is not actually moral.

There is a second factor that causes people to be homophobic. Some folk are scared by gays because their ways and attitudes strike a chord in themselves, which they don't want to recognise. It's a bit like when some men read about an act of rape, or see it on a movie. They condemn it, sometimes loudly, but something in them actually enjoys it. The evidence of surveys is that more people have homosexual thoughts, and desires, than ever act upon them. Surveys in America have come up with figures of more than 30% of men admitting they have felt sexually attracted to other men at some time in their lives. Homophobia can be a defence mechanism. We condemn loudest the demons we most fear in ourselves. Unfortunately gay people have to suffer because of that.

The Threat to Family Life

Another factor that makes evangelicals dig in their heels is the possible threat to family life. We are seeing a disintegration of the family at this time in history. It is absolutely right that Christians are concerned. The results are already much more serious that most people realise, and it is likely to get much worse. It is not impossible that it could become a key factor in the breakdown of civilisation as we have known it.

But it is not gay people who have been responsible for the break-up of families. It is straight people. The American evangelical leader Jim Wallis in *"God's Politics"* writes, "To say gay and lesbian people are responsible for the breakdown of the heterosexual family is simply wrong. That breakdown is causing a great social crisis that affects us all, but it is hardly the fault of gays and lesbians. It has very little to do with them and honestly more to do with heterosexual dysfunction and sin". He goes on, when commenting on the issue of gay marriages, "When conservatives seem to suggest that the future of western civilisation is at stake in the battle over the legal status of same-sex couples, they seriously overstate the issue".

Straight people have also been guilty, though perhaps unintentionally, of preventing gay people having the benefits of family life. By isolating them, by their attitudes, from the main-stream of society they have driven many of them into 'non-family' and so added to dysfunctionality. Gay folk, when referring to other gays, often say "She's family". They've had to produce a substitute family, the gay community, for the one they have lost.

The right-of-centre international magazine, *The Economist*, made gay marriage the subject of its main article during the 2004 American Presidential campaign. Commenting on the opposition from the religious right to gay marriage, it suggests that it was strange that there should be such an onslaught from Christians, against the idea of people wanting to make family commitments to one another, and so create homes and families. This is at a time when any kind of commitment to the home is more likely to bring stability to society than instability. *The Economist*, of course, represents a secular point of view.

Evangelicals have valid reasons for querying the concept of gay marriage. But evangelicals do need to recognise that opposition to gay practice and culture, on the grounds of defence of the family, is neither as strong an argument, or as logical an argument, as is assumed. For all the gay people who spend their time going from bar to bar, and bed to bed, there are far more whose main goal in life is just like that of any other human being, to have a partner to love and share their life with, a nice house in the suburbs, a garden, a dog and in many cases children.

Many of them would also like to go to the local church, and the golf club, and be accepted just like anyone else. The more gay people are accepted by the general community, the more likely they are to become boring middle-class suburbanites, even voting the conservative ticket in elections!

Is the Western View of Marriage Biblical?

There is a further weakness in the traditional 'Evangelical Family Values' platform; the assumption that western concepts of marriage are specifically Christian. A major contributory factor to the breakdown is that the pattern of marriage we have promoted is not particularly Biblical or Christian.

There are strong Biblical arguments for the arranged marriage, though not enforced marriage. The divorce rate is much lower in those societies and cultures which follow the arranged marriage practice. African Christians in particular would point out how limited the western idea of family is. The extended family pattern of much of the third world is far more Biblical, and provides far more care, support and security for all. The gay community has been forced to create its own expression of family life because so many gay people have been prevented from enjoying normal family life, or normal church life. I have found this community sometimes to be more caring and supportive.

As Originally Given

There is one last, and important issue, that causes evangelical Christians to resist change. It's because of our strong convictions about what Jude in his letter calls 'the Faith that was once entrusted to the saints'. Jude calls upon us to 'contend' for it. Our belief that there is a 'body of truth' which was once and for all given, by what we call revelation, puts us in the freaks class in the post-modern era, and dangerous freaks at that. Dogma in the religious realm, and ideology in the political, are very much 'out'. But not for evangelicals.

So change in beliefs is always viewed with a good deal of suspicion. We have seen too many shifts in the past, that have then led to another shift, and eventually the undermining of the Gospel. Evangelicals are people with firm beliefs as to what the Gospel is. We believe the Bible to be 'God breathed' (2 Timothy 3:16) and our guide for doctrine and conduct. I subscribe wholly to that belief. Throughout my Christian life and ministry I have been known as a fighter when it comes to the fundamentals of Christian belief. I have put my neck on the chopping block on a number of occasions, risking my ministry and livelihood for the sake of my doctrinal beliefs.

In that respect I am undoubtedly at the conservative end of the evangelical spectrum. I've already said, in this chapter, that I am very concerned at the way evangelicals are becoming woolly in their views of the exclusivity of God's way of salvation, that it is through Christ alone. I am just as disturbed by the even wider tendency to question the eternal nature of future punishment. But I believe it is also important to distinguish between what is fundamental and clear, and what is secondary and not yet fully clear, between what cannot be changed and what sometimes needs to be changed.

The fact is that there are many issues on which evangelicals have come to a fresh understanding of what Scripture teaches over the years. The seventeenth century Puritan John Robinson, who pastored the folk who embarked on the Mayflower to become the founders of modern America, made the famous statement "The Lord has yet more light and truth to show forth from his Word". Robinson was an evangelical, who was prepared to leave his own country rather than give up his beliefs, but he did not believe that we have yet fully understood all the Bible has to say to us. There is such a thing as 'progressive revelation'.

Key to the 16th century Protestant Reformation was the belief that the church has to go on being reformed by the Word of God, and this involves a continuing and progressive enlightenment by the Holy Spirit. A close examination of church history shows that this is precisely what has happened. The Reformation itself had at its heart a renewed and fuller understanding of the key doctrine of Justification through faith alone.

In the 17th century the Holy Spirit seems to have focused on the doctrine of the Church, and many Christians were willing to suffer for their fuller understanding, including those who sailed on the Mayflower. The Wesleyan revival of the 18th century saw a fresh emphasis on the work of the Holy Spirit and the need for a life of holiness. In the nineteenth century there was a focus on the Great Commission, the near return of the Lord Jesus Christ, and the social implications of the Gospel.

The enlightening of the church by the Holy Spirit has continued in our time. The so-called Charismatic Renewal has had an immense impact on the church of God throughout the world and has been key to the greatest expansion of the Gospel in

Christian history. But most evangelicals agonised over the theology at the heart of it, to begin with. The battle was hard and long over the teaching of the "Baptism in the Holy Spirit", and whether or not supernatural gifts of the Spirit are for today.

I was personally involved in a long inward struggle, and then an outward one when I began to share and preach my own change of thinking. The battle is to a great extent now over. There is a consensus amongst most Evangelicals as to what Scripture teaches. There is no doubt that this has involved a distinct shift in our understanding, application and experience of what it teaches. Accompanying that has been a new understanding of the Church and the ministries in the Church.

There is now a much greater understanding of the Church as an organism, as against the overemphasis on its organisation. This has led to a marked shift from one-man leadership, clerically dominated worship, to a much fuller exercise of the ministry and priesthood of all believers. When this shift first began to take place many feared some of the consequences. Some felt that the exercise of such gifts as tongues and prophecy would lead to an undermining of Scripture, and that greater lay leadership would lead to a weakening of authority in the church. Few looking back would deny that we really were being led by the Holy Spirit to a better understanding of Scripture.

But has all the change come as a result of a change in our understanding of the Bible, motivated by the Holy Spirit? I think we have to be honest and admit that some of it has been influenced by changes in society. Society is much less formal and hierarchical than it used to be. The post second world war baby-boomer generation was the catalyst to a whole new laid-back and egalitarian informality, that is also reflected in changes in church structures, culture and worship.

Changed Views of Eschatology

There has been a distinct shift on the very contentious issue of eschatology. We were all once neatly boxed as pre-post or a-millennialists and spent enormous energy fighting for our corner. But many main-stream evangelicals have become dissatisfied with those over-simplified categorisations. The fact that evangelical Christians, equally committed to the authority of Scripture, can differ so much suggests that we have not yet come to a full understanding of what the Bible teaches.

Many of us now believe that the approaches we took in the past were not always helpful. Now we put less emphasis on the either/or and a lot more on the already/and the not yet. Is the future on this earth all gloom and doom, as pre-millennialists seem to say, or is it bright with promise as post-millennialists seem to think? The answer is probably 'both'. The darkness and light will increase alongside each other, until the day of Christ's coming.

Is the Kingdom of God here and now or does it only come after Christ's return? Most would now say that the Kingdom of God breaks through in history, will increasingly break through in blessing in this last stage of history, but it will only fully come after Christ's return. All can agree that the Kingdom will come on earth, even though we may still be divided as to whether it is this earth or a renewed earth.

This represents a marked change in our understanding of what Scripture teaches, and most would see that as beneficial in its effects. But again, the changes have not come for theological reasons alone. Post-modern man is not very interested in the past or the future. He is interested in what works and happens now. So present day Christians are more interested in manifestations of the Kingdom now than our forefathers were.

Women in the Church

Another important change has been in the role of women in the church. Forty years ago evangelicals would have been near unanimous in believing that women should not hold positions which involved 'headship', in other words being in authority over men. Therefore a woman might be a full-time church worker but not a senior pastor in charge of a congregation, and not a ruling elder. We would have based that attitude on our understanding of Scripture teaching.

It is still a very contentious issue, and the battle over the interpretation of the relevant Scriptures is still fiercely fought, and to me finely balanced. But the fact is that there has been an enormous change in practice and the majority of evangelicals, in Britain, seem to favour that change. They would attribute that change to a 'better' understanding of Scripture. All the major Protestant denominations now have women functioning in lead roles on the same basis as men.

The truth is that many churches would have to close down if it were not so. Even those of us who still have reservations, and I am one of them, have to admit that male prejudice often denied women their full role in ministry in God's church. But have all these changes come about through the Holy Spirit leading us into a fresh understanding of the Bible? No. Scripture is supposed to come first, but I doubt if it did. There is no question that social pressures, and the feminist movement, have had an enormous impact on our thinking and our actions.

Divorce

When it comes to moral issues evangelicals have had to wrestle very hard with the matter of divorce. Faced with massive changes in the attitudes of society, which inevitably get reflected in the church, we have searched the Scriptures for help. We still see clear principles laid down that we feel we must uphold and seek to apply. But when it comes to details we are sometimes met with silence in Scripture, with no guidelines to give us the answers to complex situations.

I am primarily a pastor/teacher not a theologian or scholar. I am grateful to theologians who keep our minds focused on the primacy of the truths of Scripture. But having spent almost forty-five years pastoring and counselling people struggling with marriage problems I frequently find myself floundering trying to find the right answers for particular situations.

Most evangelicals, in practice, opt for a compassionate approach where we are unsure. We want to be seen as a caring community. We are also aware that the day may come when we are in need of the same compassion. But pastors often live with an uneasy conscience as to whether we did the right thing in particular cases. Some of our decisions come back to haunt us. But there is no going back to a day when it seemed much clearer, but in fact was sometimes over-simplified and even cruel.

We have to live with and deal with the world of today, the world as we find it. We do our best in a quagmire of relativism. We have many more divorced folk in our congregations than we used to have. An increasing number of pastors and full-time church workers have been divorced, without relinquishing their ministries. Most of us don't like it, but we have come to terms with it.

Wine, Women & Song

The same is true of a lot of secondary issues on which there has been change. Forty years ago it was taboo for most evangelicals to drink even the smallest amount of alcohol, go to the cinema, even watch television, go dancing or for women to wear make-up. Sunday was a strict sabbath. Even in my non-Christian home I was made to wear a Sunday suit as a child, whilst most games-playing was very restricted.

Amongst the sexual taboos, masturbation was definitely of the devil and would lead to considerable psychological damage. Many of us have come to re-think this one and now see it as something which can be a 'lesser evil' ; especially for those faced with the complexities of the single life through no fault of their own.

All this was part of our evangelical inheritance from the Puritans and the Victorians.   But we would have claimed Scripture support for most of this.   It's easy to smile now but we took those taboos seriously enough to judge other people by them. Fortunately we've learned better. We now leave it to each person's conscience because we no longer believe that Scripture draws that kind of line.   Scripture is not a manual that gives us the answers on all the issues which arise in contemporary culture.   Romans 14 makes clear that there are 'grey' areas on which Christians can come to different convictions.   What matters is that we each live out our lives conscious that we are answerable to God, and that we do not judge other Christians.

In view of all the changes that have taken place, why is it that many evangelicals refuse to even take a second-look at the gay issue?   What if time should prove we have been too harsh? What of all the misery and pain we continue to inflict on gay people? Can we justify it if there is any doubt as to whether we are doing God's will?

Alienation

Traditional views have not only alienated many gay people to the Gospel but will increasingly alienate non-Christians, for whom homosexuality is no longer a moral issue. Last Sunday, after I had preached at a neighbouring church, I was introduced to a lady who her friend described as a definite non-Christian. She had only come to church because she had been dragged there by this friend she was visiting. The woman said that her problem, with the Christian Church and message, was that

82

throughout history the Church had always come over as 'very fierce'.

I think that's how most Christians see the Muslim religion. We admire some of the uprightness and faith of Muslims, but we sense a lack of compassion and a view of God that is remote and very fierce. Yet so often that's how evangelicals appear to society. We are even lumped together with Muslims, and politically extreme Jews, as part of the 'Fundamentalist problem' at the present time.

The non-Christian world does not see the Jesus who seemed to prefer being with the very irreligious of his day rather than the religious. There has always been a compelling attraction about the person of Jesus, that somehow the world doesn't see in us. Most of us know all this, so we turn up our 'loving the sinner but hating the sin' rhetoric. But it doesn't really convince people because we don't come across as loving gay people. At best we are very uncomfortable with them. We are too scared of them to love them; scared of what they might do to us and our religion if we give way too much.

Yes, we must defend Christian standards but let's be careful that we don't have a lop-sided view of what those standards are. What if time, and maybe even the work of the Holy Spirit, reveals to us that we have not properly understood what it means to be gay, and what the Bible says on the subject, and we have not even *tried* to understand better? What if our resistance to change is based on prejudice more than on principle? I believe the day will come when many more evangelical Christians will feel ashamed of their prejudice and blindness, and ashamed of the way they have failed gay people.

Some Contemporary Evangelical Views

Let me finish by quoting a couple of contemporary evangelical writers. Philip Yancey in his runaway best-seller *"What's so amazing about Grace?"* refers to his friend Mel White, who I've already described. White shook the evangelical world when he came out as gay. Yancey was allowed to read through some of the hate-mail White had received from Christians. "I could barely make my way through the letters. The pages were septic with hatred. In the name of God, writers rained down curses and profanity and threats. I kept wanting to protest: 'Wait, Mel is my friend. You don't know him'. To the letter writers though, Mel was a label - *pervert* - not a person". He goes on to describe White's Christ-like reaction to much of the vilification.

Richard Lovelace is another American evangelical writer who has produced some tremendous books, including a classic on Revival. In 1997 he wrote, "Most of the repenting that needs to be done on this issue of homosexuality needs to be done by straight people, including straight Christians. By far the greater sin in our churches is the sin of neglect, fear, hatred - just wanting to brush these people under the rug".

Tony Campolo - "I am not asking that Christians gloss over Biblical teachings, nor that we justify same-gender eroticism. I am simply reminding Christians that we are supposed to love people - even those we have been socially conditioned to despise".

Chapter Four - Nature or Nurture ?

What Causes Homosexuality?

Some of you will be asking, "Yes, but what about what the Bible says?" Clearly that is a key question for Christians. But first we need to get a better understanding of homosexuality and what causes it, because that will considerably affect how we approach the Bible passages we deal with.

The traditional understanding of the Biblical texts has been based on the belief that homosexuality finds its roots in nurture and choice. Whether we like it or not expert opinion no longer believes that. Researches into the causes of homosexuality more and more lean to the view that for some people, at least, it is nature not nurture that is the prime cause. The overwhelming evidence is that there is a small, but significant section of people found in every nation or culture that is born gay.

Those evangelicals who disagree with this are becoming increasingly isolated and will become more so. I believe they resist this change because they know it will affect their interpretation of Scripture. All of us have pre-conceptions which affect how we understand the Bible, including me right now.

Unfortunately for both sides of the argument there is no simple answer as to what causes homosexuality. Michael Vasey, an Anglican evangelical who lectured at St. John's College Durham, quotes in his helpful book *"Strangers and Friends"* Pope Paul VI as saying "Burning questions are also complex ones. We should have respect for the complexity of things, listen, weigh them".

Over-simplification of the issues is a major cause of some of the traditional evangelical pronouncements on homosexuality. There was a letter in my daily newspaper yesterday condemning a pro-gay article the previous day. The writer was obviously an evangelical Christian. The letter was embarrassing. It began "I am neither a qualified theologian nor do I have a degree in theology, but it takes neither to understand what the Bible says about homosexuals, bisexuals or transgendered people. The act is an abomination in God's sight and there are a number of Scriptures to back this up". The writer carries on at considerable length and with great certainty that he knows God's mind.

Every bigot who stands with placards at Gay Pride Parades 'knows' with absolute certainty what God says. How I wish it was so simple. We live in a day when people want answers but unfortunately sound-bite answers.

I was recently accused of being evasive on this subject because I hesitated with some of my answers when critically questioned. You will be disappointed in this book if you are expecting clear cut answers to all your questions. I don't have the answers to many of the questions, including some of the big ones. Why am I writing, then? Because I believe there are good grounds for challenging some of the traditional answers, and I write also in the hope that I can make some suggestions for a fresh approach. I am concerned to get us out of the present log-jam, because our failure is causing hurt to a lot of people.

Is it 'Either Or'?

Probably the most accurate answer at this point in time, as to whether it is nurture or nature, is to say "both may come into it". Martin Hallet heads up a Christian counselling service for people struggling with homosexuality called the "True Freedom

Trust". He writes with experience of that struggle and approaches it from a compassionate, but fairly traditional point of view.

He puts a lot of emphasis on post-natal conditioning experience, in other words nurture. But he also writes "I firmly believe that our sexual orientation is a product of a highly complex process of human experiences and development. The roots of this development process are found very early on in childhood. There may well be some *genetic component* (italics mine) which helps to set us on the road towards developing sexually. But even this is difficult to determine for sure. This is because we are born with up to nine months of experience within the womb. As a part of our mother's body, we have received messages, both positive and negative, about ourselves and our environment, from our mother's emotions. It must be appreciated that everyone's experience of life is different, and so is the response to it. This means that just as our personality is as unique as a fingerprint, so is our sexuality. I don't believe anyone can give a clear blueprint of sexual development, but we can find signposts which help point towards the process of development" (from a pamphlet *"How Does it all Begin?"*).

He goes on to speak of the importance of early affirmation and unconditional love from both parents, and then puts forward the argument made by most people who believe the prime cause of homosexuality is nurture. "As a boy, my relationship with my father will be especially important in terms of establishing my sense of self-worth, and identity, as a male. As a girl I will need the same kind of affirmation from my mother".

I do not deny for one moment that this parental bonding is important, and may well play a decisive part in the development of sexual orientation with some people. But if this is the key factor, why is it that there is little evidence in support from the large number of children who are at the present time being brought up in single parent homes? The present breakdown in family life is partly due to a high divorce rate. But it's also because of the growing number of people who want children but not marriage commitment, or even a permanent partner sometimes.

With so many children being brought up without the traditional two parents we ought to have clear evidence for the nurture argument. We would expect to find a lot more children from single parent homes growing up with homosexual tendencies. We would expect a higher percentage of gay people coming from single parent homes. But there are no statistics that I am aware of that support that idea.

Support for my argument comes from other cultures. There is a great deal more emphasis on the traditional family in African culture than in present-day western culture. The extended family is the norm, where children are very rarely without a whole support group of not only two parents, but grandparents, and brothers and sisters, and a lot of others who westerners would barely recognise as relatives. It's a situation in which there is plenty of opportunity to bond naturally with male and female. But homosexuality is still common, though often not so obvious because it is much harder to 'come-out' in African culture.

During the period when democracy came to South Africa a black gay pastor appeared on a panel discussion on homosexuality on TV. It was a 'first' for South Africa. I met him some months later. He told me that after the broadcast he was contacted by more than forty closeted black gay ministers.

Fresh evidence for my argument that homosexuality is primarily from nature continues to come in even as I write. A friend of mine, Dr John Maasch, pointed me to a series of articles published in the Boston Globe that summarise very helpfully the arguments. They point out that for a long time prejudice against homosexuals blocked the kind of funding needed to do extensive research, but that situation is changing as public opinion changes. John Maasch works in a brain injury rehabilitation unit in New Zealand. He is an evangelical

Christian with firm convictions but his researches have convinced him that whatever the final answers as to the causes of homosexuality, the overwhelming evidence is that they are pre-natal.

Choice

Hallett and others argue that whatever the pre-natal or post-natal conditioning, it is our response to it that makes the difference. In other words the *choices* we make. My own personal experience denies that.

There is no question that there were factors in my nurture that could well have played a part in my future development. My mother had sexual problems of her own and there was an imbalance in the parenting roles. But at no point in my growing years, or early adult years, was I influenced by homosexuals. As I've described earlier, from teen years I was a very earnest Christian who tried to live a godly life. All the instincts of a gay man were there, though I did not understand them, but I did not act on them.

I tried to date girls and had ample opportunity to develop natural relationship with women and marry. I was regarded as a 'good catch' and needed my wits about me to deal with the number of would-be suitors! But it didn't happen for me. I didn't even understand why until I was in my thirties. Not until my fifties did I begin to have regular contact with the gay community and learn about gay life.

Two weeks ago I counselled a gay man in his late forties. He worshipped in one of my churches from time to time when he was a theological student, more than twenty-five years ago. I was a fiery Calvinistic preacher and drew many students from some very conservative Bible colleges, who wanted to learn from me. He told me that even then he recognised I was gay. Whatever traits or mannerisms gave me away could not have been learned from other gay people. I had no regular contact with them that I know of.

It is only in fairly recent years that the general public has come to accept that homosexuality stems more from nature than nurture. But this opinion began to predominate in the medical and academic world as long as fifty years ago. It was that change in thinking which led to major changes in the law. It seems extraordinary to us now that people were once given prison sentences for nothing more than same sex acts, between two individuals, in the privacy of their own homes. There are many parts of the world where it is still true.

A Criminal Offence

Persecution of gays was prominent in Hitler's Germany. The pink triangle has become a gay symbol, but it was Hitler who first introduced it, to mark out gays in his concentrations camps. Persecution of gays is still found in Africa, as well as the Caribbean, and of course Muslim dominated countries. Homosexual acts may be a sin but that doesn't make them a crime.

There has been considerable resurgence of interest, in recent years, in the life and works of Oscar Wilde. His books have a healthy sale. His plays are performed frequently and have been made into movies. He is regarded as one of the great figures of English literature. It is hard to realise that only a hundred years ago he was imprisoned, in Reading jail, for homosexual offences, with a sentence of hard labour from which he never really recovered. It brought about his early death.

We realise how big the change has been when we remind ourselves that Sir Ian McKellen, for a long time Britain's leading Shakesperian actor, and now a movie star, is an openly gay man. And he suffers no apparent negative consequences. That may well reflect the decline of faith and morals in Britain, but even conservative Christians would think it absurd to sentence him to hard labour for consenting sexual acts.

The Wolfenden Report of 1957 was the catalyst that led to changes in Britain, particularly the 1967 Sexual Offences Act that legalised homosexual acts conducted in private. The report accepted the view that 'there exists in certain persons a homosexual propensity'.

Once it was accepted that homosexuality is not simply a matter of perverse choice it was no longer possible to treat it as a criminal offence. But it took another ten years for Parliament to act upon it because with the general public it was still a political hot potato. The failure to understand the causes of homosexuality still made it a thing of dark horror in many people's minds. But as early as 1955 the British Medical Association had published a memorandum which distinguished between *'essential'* homosexuality and *'acquired'* homosexuality.

Even some evangelical theologians were beginning to have second thoughts. The distinguished German preacher-theologian Helmut Thielicke wrote, in 1964, that he had come to accept the view that constitutional homosexuality was "largely unsusceptible to medical or psychotherapeutic treatment". In 1974, M G Barker, an evangelical Christian who was a psychiatrist, wrote a booklet for the Christian Medical Fellowship which supported Thielicke's view.

Catholics have traditionally been as opposed to accepting homosexual practice as Evangelicals. But in 1972 a Catholic theologian, Charles Curran, agreed with Thielicke and went further saying he "accepted that in general the homosexual is not responsible for his condition and that celibacy and sublimation are not always possible or even desirable". "Therapy" he said "does not offer great promise. There are many somewhat stable homosexual unions which afford their partners some human fulfilment and contentment. Obviously such unions are better than homosexual promiscuity". While attempt should be made, Curran believed, to overcome the condition if possible, "at times one may reluctantly accept the compromise that homosexual unions are the only way in which some people can find a satisfying degree of humanity".

Once it began to be accepted that there were people who had no choice concerning their sexual disposition, there had to be some fresh thinking concerning their legitimate needs as human beings. Evangelicals like things to be clear cut. But applying the Gospel to human conditions, as we find them rather than as we would like them to be, is often messy, and theologically and spiritually unsatisfying.

A Mental Disorder?

Thinking had changed to such an extent by the nineteen-seventies that medical opinion had begun to respond to it more strongly. In 1973 the trustees of the American Psychiatric Association dropped homosexuality from the list of recognised mental disorders. "Some of the Association felt that this was an unscientific concession to the rising political and social pressures of organised homosexuals, but the action was upheld in 1974 by a large majority of the Association" (David Atkinson - *"Homosexuals in the Christian Fellowship"*). The World Health Organisation made a similar decision.

Michael Vasey, in his book, comments that these decisions were not made as a 'result of some liberal conspiracy', they represented the recognition that there is nothing intrinsic to homosexual orientation that makes it psychologically disordered. "If homosexual people have difficulty functioning in society this is not a result of their personal instability but of society's unwillingness to accept their orientation".

We shall see when we look at gay culture, in the next chapter, that many of the things that make the gay community objectionable to straight people are themselves reactions to that lack of acceptance. Treating homosexual people as unacceptably different has to some extent made them different.

Even the title 'gay' as against 'homosexual' marks the assertion by gay people of the right to name themselves. Society in general has now adopted that description.

Many evangelical Christians like to keep the more negative connotation of the word 'homosexual'. I have faced criticism from evangelical friends for using the word 'gay' of myself. I do it, in part to stress that being homosexual is not primarily what you do, but what you are. Being celibate does not change what or who I am.

Kinsey's Rating Scale

At this point I need to make some distinctions, because the term 'gay' has become an umbrella term that covers a number of categories of people. I am not trying to put a case for all who come under that umbrella.

The Kinsey reports on human sexuality, published in 1948 and 1953, formed the basis of much of the debate of the last fifty years. But one section I find particularly helpful and relevant in understanding the range of sexual experience. Kinsey's researches in the USA came up with the surprising finding that 37% of the male population claimed to have engaged in at least some overt homosexual experience to the point of orgasm, between the start of adolescence and old age. Four per cent of all males claimed to be exclusively homosexual throughout their lives, after the onset of adolescence.

He proposed a scale to encompass this broad range of sexual experience, a heterosexual-homosexual rating scale between 0 (exclusively heterosexual with no homosexual tendencies) to 6 (exclusively homosexual). Amongst his conclusions was that the majority of men come between 1- 5, i.e. are neither exclusively heterosexual or exclusively homosexual.

This makes sense of my own counselling and researches. I am almost certainly a Kinsey 6. I do not feel attracted to, or feel capable of, sex with women. But numbers of actively gay men I know, whose predominant attraction is quite definitely to men, have had sex with women. This is obvious from the number of men who are, or have been, married to the opposite sex but over a period of time have found that position untenable.

I have referred to a friend, who is a strong Christian, who was actively homosexual in his teens, then married and has been married for well over twenty years. He has two adult children. But his predominant desire sexually is still for men and from time to time he lapses - much to his grief I might add. He is adamant that he is not bisexual (that is, equally attracted to both sexes), and says his wife is the only woman he has ever felt attracted to physically. He would probably be rated 5 on Kinsey's scale.

Those in the middle, the 3's and 4's,are the most difficult for me to understand. I do not doubt that there are people who are genuinely bisexual. I have talked to sincere, honest, struggling people - one or two of them evangelical ministers, who say they are equally attracted to both sexes. But I cannot think of any grounds for them engaging in both kinds of sex. I understand very well the Christian, who has a predominant and strong attraction to the same sex, who finds it very difficult to be celibate. But it seems to me that a Christian who has an equal attraction to both sexes must choose what is clearly the Biblical norm, sex with one person of the opposite sex in a relationship of marriage. You cannot have your cake and eat it as well.

In some recent researches, in which a sizeable group of men who claimed to be bisexual were shown provocative pictures of males and females, a decisive majority were sexually aroused more by the male images. In the stages of 'coming-out', some men choose to call themselves 'bisexual' because they think it is more acceptable to their friends and society. There are some well-known examples of celebrities doing this.

With all these variations it is not surprising that heterosexual Christians get confused when they hear people like me pleading for a more sympathetic and accommodating attitude to gays in the church. They think of well know movie stars who have their 'lesbian moments', characters in TV soaps and dramas who change sides when it suits them, sexual orgies, and Gay Pride celebrations on TV newscasts where cross-dressing and sexual exposure are pushed in your face.

How do we Categorise Gay People?

So it needs to be clarified who I am pleading for. There are five categories of people that tend to come under the general label 'gay'.

First there are what someone has called 'Same sex adventurers'. They are not homosexual but heterosexuals who engage in homosexual acts. Obvious examples are teenagers in Boarding Schools, who engage in same sex acts as part of their sexual discovery, and because there are no available girls/boys around. There's a similar situation with those in the military or in prison.

A friend of mine died not long ago and he died of AIDS. He had been imprisoned for several years and I believe he was raped during that time. It is a scandal, to me, that he appears not to have received anti-retroviral drugs. Also in this category are the people I've referred to in the entertainment world, and promiscuous people in general, who in today's moral climate seek sex any way they can get it. In this moral climate there are those who find it kinky to engage in same-sex acts. Men, in particular, are 'turned on' by watching women performing sexual acts. These really are 'unnatural acts'.

Secondly there are bisexual people. No more needs to be added about them.

Thirdly, there are transgendered people who are not strictly gay, but get included in people's thinking about the gay community. They are people who have the characteristics of one sex but claim the psychological characteristics of the other, and undergo surgery to rectify that. I mentioned earlier a large evangelical church which asked my advice when a transgendered person applied for membership. The man was a sincere Christian and committed to involvement in the church.

Fourthly there are people struggling with their sexuality, and have had same-sex experience, but are not true homosexuals. The same-sex attraction in their case is a result of nurture factors, or gay culturalisation. They may have come under the strong influence of an older man. They may even have taken up prostitution, to make money, without being truly gay. The time comes when they desire to live a heterosexual life and with help a significant change can be brought about. As we shall see later there is good evidence to suggest that the reference in 1 Corinthians 6, to homosexuality, is referring to these two situations just mentioned, the older man and homosexual prostitution. It is probably what Paul had in mind when in 1 Corinthians 6:11 he says to some members of the Corinthian Church; "And that is what some of you were".

The fifth type is what I will call the true homosexual. They have always had a primary attraction to the same sex. It is part of who they are. A further distinction needs to be made in this fifth group between those who have a homosexual orientation but don't engage in sexual acts with other people, and those who do. The former desire to do so, fantasise about doing so, but don't actually do it. It may be for religious reasons, but it may simply be lack or opportunity or fear. Surveys have shown that a fair number of gay men who are active, do not like or engage in anal intercourse.

Sometimes people tell me stories of people they know, who they say have been 'delivered' from homosexuality. They do it to convince me that my views on the subject are wrong. I always tell them that I cannot respond to the point they are making without meeting the people concerned and listening to their stories.

It's the same when people come to me for counselling. I first want to listen to their story. Tony Campolo rightly makes the point that "no two homosexuals are homosexual for exactly the same reasons or causes". He goes on to say "What makes matters even more confusing is that, based on research that I have done, I believe that what forms the male homosexual orientation may be very different from what forms the female sexual orientation".

Helping Lesbians

Which raises a question I need to answer. Most of my female readers will have become very aware that I am dealing with this subject mostly from a male point of view. I may well be hurting and disappointing lesbians who read this book. Why have I chosen to take this path?

Firstly, because I'm writing much of it from a personal perspective. I feel incompetent to write from the woman's point of view.

Secondly, because the Bible deals with it mainly as a male issue, and a primary reason for writing is to deal with homosexuality from a Biblical perspective. Only Romans 1 specifically includes the female.

Thirdly because I agree with Campolo, that there are sharp differences between the gay male situation and the female situation, as well as similarities. Both have suffered from the prejudice and hatred of society. Women in general have also suffered a great deal from abuse at the hands of men. This is one reason, in my opinion, why some women are in lesbian relationships. They are not lesbian by orientation, but because of abuse from men they have turned to other women for intimacy and fulfilment. In some respects it is easier for women to have relationships with other women than it is for men to have relationships with men.

In most churches there are more unmarried women than men. This is often because there have not been Christian men for them to marry. They remain single out of faithfulness to God. But this also makes it easier for a woman, who is unmarried because she is a lesbian, than it is for a gay man. Singleness for a man automatically makes him suspect. Two women can share a home together much more easily than two men. So it is more common for Christian women to live together, sometimes through their entire adult life. They may be lesbians, they may not be. I suspect that the relationship is often not clearly defined. It is acceptable for women to show affection towards one another in a way that it is not for men. It's one of the reasons I think why statistics usually give a lower figure for the number of women who identify themselves as homosexual.

The picture is further blurred because the sex act plays a less important part in the life of the average woman. Some women will regard my comment as very sexist. It is certainly a generalisation and generalisations are regarded as politically incorrect. But forty years of pastoral and marriage counselling convinces me it's true. Women tend to enjoy the things that lead up to the sex act more than the act itself. My lesbian boss in California once jokingly said to me, "I think about sex maybe twice a day. They tell me that men do it on average about every seven seconds!" When I say that to men they normally grin sheepishly and nod.

There's another joke that has more than an element of truth. "In a heterosexual marriage it's the woman who puts the brakes on. In a gay male relationship there are no brakes". It is part of the problem. My guess is that for women their sexual orientation is less clearly defined. Just as some in apparently lesbian relationships are not really lesbians, there are a good many who are lesbian and in a lesbian relationship, but don't know it. It is not sufficiently clearly defined.

The Christian Lesbian Dilemma

So the issues affecting gay men are different from those affecting women. But there are basic issues common to both. I quote from a letter from a lesbian friend, a professional woman who is a strong and faithful Christian. I have known her over a long period of time and have been her pastor and counsellor. She writes, "My main reason for coming to see you, and my main reason for writing now, is to seek your counsel, which I know to be godly, wise and experienced, on the issue which currently dominates my life to an unhealthy degree; that of coming to terms with being gay. I have recently become quite ill with a duodenal ulcer, and I know that a huge part of it is my inner conflict. I have prayed endlessly, sought God and struggled with this thing for over fifteen years now, and it won't go away...it fact it's getting much stronger. The small amount of counsel I have received has either been from gay people (which is decidedly ungodly, as you can imagine. Yet so much of it rings true to me and I have to acknowledge that). Or counsel from Christians, who have never experienced what it means to be gay, is 'godly' but totally misses the reality. Hence the inner turmoil".

She goes on "Over the past ten years I have had love relationships with three women which became sexual; all the time denying that what was happening, was happening. As a result I have lost all three friendships; they just couldn't take the conflict, and the worst thing is that the last two women have abandoned the church and Christianity...mainly because of how destructive the whole thing was...and I do feel responsible for some of that. They are both women who I still love deeply and their rejecting Jesus is tremendously painful...hence my conflict which exists at the most fundamental level. My relationship with Jesus, and all that entails; God is my Creator and Father, I am filled with the Holy Spirit and He blesses me with gifts, I believe in the Church and that God's plan is for the church and for me to be involved in a church. These things are non-negotiable...they are the basis of my life. My relationship with God has never been better in a way; He speaks tenderly and has been leading me in other areas; I have a hunger for His Word and to pray, that I have never had before...I have a strong sense of God's calling on my life...I am currently leading a house church...I even teach at a Bible School".

She goes on to describe how she had been allowed to do these things in an evangelical church because she was no longer in a relationship. But the conflict had only got stronger. "My commitment to God's Word and what it says about homosexuality, versus my instinctive knowledge of God's love are causing me enormous conflict and I don't really know where to go from here. My prime concern is God and what he says. On the surface the options are i) deny it, try and get married, and end up 'accepted' and miserable; ii) accept it and resign myself to a life of restricted relationships and celibacy. To me I would rather die than live that conflict and I have told God that. I admire so much your ability to walk that path, but I would honestly rather go to heaven now. I am an intensely people-oriented person and the times when I have been in a deeply intimate and loving relationship have eclipsed by far any other experience in my life. iii) The third option is to stop pretending and be who I am, walk in the light and follow my heart. I'm terrified of where I'll end up though, because almost certainly I'll fall in love with another woman".

The letter was written several years ago. I met her again recently, with her partner, a beautiful Christian woman. She is still following God strongly and doing her best to be involved in an evangelical church. She is clearly an example of someone for whom celibacy is not an option. Someone of weaker character and weaker faith would have given up the struggle long ago. She would either have given up on evangelical churches, or would probably have given up practising her faith altogether. That's what most people in her position do. Or she might have committed suicide, which is what some do. It cannot be right that good people are forced to make that kind of choice.

Exodus Ministries

I refer again to Tony Campolo. He is in a rare position, because he is straight, because of his evangelical credentials and because of the considerable researches and involvement, with his wife, in counselling gay people. He still believes that the Bible does not allow same-sex erotic relationships, but is convinced that some better way ahead has to be found. In a chapter in his book *"Speaking my mind"* he shares all his concerns, and uncertainties but then makes these comments; "There is one thing of which I am convinced, and that is that homosexuals do not choose their orientation. Whatever the causal factors may be, I am sure that the imprinting of the orientation occurs so early in the biological/social/psychological development of the person that he or she can never recall having made a conscious choice."

That conviction marks the dividing line between those evangelicals who continue to hold the traditional position, and those who think there has to be a change of thinking, that leads to a change of action by churches. Campolo goes on "Evangelical Christians generally support the belief that change in sexual orientation is possible. Consequently they call upon homosexuals to seek the help that they believe is required for transformation into heterosexuals. A whole array of ministries has sprung up that have as their mission to help homosexuals to become straight. Together these ministries are incorporated into a loosely connected organisation called Exodus". He goes on to describe how the ministry of the Exodus grouping encourages those who have benefited from their ministry to give testimonies to their healing and change, and then says "These testimonies come across as sincere and convincing; nevertheless, there are questions to be raised about them".

He raises the issue of the number of leaders in the Exodus ministries, who are no longer with Exodus because their so-called cure did not hold, to which I've referred earlier. I have mentioned my doctor friend who had been a leader with an Exodus-related ministry. I have been involved in trying to pick up the pieces of people who have gone through the courses, and been declared to be changed people. They are usually people who desperately wanted to be changed and so the disappointment is often overwhelming.

Campolo expresses the opinion that most of those who claim that they have been changed from homosexuals into heterosexuals are in fact bisexuals. In other words they are somewhere in the middle on Kinsey's scale. I am sure there are people with a homosexual tendency who can get married and remain married. But that puts them in a very different position from the genuine homosexual who has known no other orientation or attraction.

Campolo ends "It is my own belief that change is possible, but not likely. Because I believe in a God who works miracles, I cannot discount the possibility of change. Furthermore, while there are doubts in my mind about some of the testimonies I have heard from ex-gays, I am not so cynical as to discount all of them. On the other hand, of the hundreds of deeply religious gay males I interviewed while on the faculty of the University of Pennsylvania, I found that all of them had desperately sought change at one time or another. Sadly, all of them had met with only frustration and disillusionment".

John McNeill in his book *"The Church and the Homosexual"* adds even weightier evidence. McNeill is a Roman Catholic priest, who was disciplined for his views by his church. He has spent years pastoring, and counselling gay people. In the first edition of his book, written thirty years ago, McNeill while taking what was then a radical position for a Roman Catholic, made this statement. "Practically all authorities agree that the first goal of counselling should be to guide the person with a homosexual problem to a heterosexual adjustment whenever possible". But he goes on to say, even at that time, two things:

    (a) ***there are real dangers in pursuing this course.*** He writes "Several moral problems face the counsellor who accepts as the primary goal to lead the homosexual to a heterosexual adjustment. Among these is the problem of the danger of fostering false hopes of a change in sexual orientation in the mind of the homosexual. Despite the optimism of some psychiatrists concerning the possibilities of change, there is little real hope that change will be effected in the practical order for a large majority of the cases of true homosexuality."

(b) **there is a low chance of success.** He quotes the statistics of some very thorough researchers. Irving Bieber, in his work *"Homosexuality; A Psychoanalytic Study",* after hundreds of work-hours by a team of researchers, concluded that only 27% of his patients changed their orientation under optimum conditions. He wrote "The writers are acquainted with hundreds of young men and women, and many older ones as well, who spent thousands of hard-earned dollars and hundreds of uncomfortable hours, seeking to overcome their imperious deviant desires, but in vain". He suggests that a more than 70% failure rate is very high, and gives little support to those who encourage homosexuals to seek change. Particularly as some of those who reported change, may well have been in Kinsey's middle range.

McNeill's book continued to be reprinted but in later editions he reports a marked change in his thinking. He reports that in the fifteen year gap between the two editions, his work and ministry to gay people as a psychotherapist and pastor has changed his view as to gay people seeking a change of sexual orientation. He writes of the very real dangers to people who attempt to deny or repress their homosexuality and live out a heterosexual life. I know that for me personally it was a tremendous relief when I stopped my more than twenty years of denial. It was like a great burden rolling off my shoulders.

McNeill concludes, in his revised book "After fifteen years of extensive therapeutic work with lesbians and gay clients, I would no longer claim there is a 'limited chance of a therapeutic cure', I now believe it is impossible to change one's sexual orientation any more than one can change blue eyes to brown. The best response one can make to one's sexual orientation is to accept it and learn to live with it in the healthiest and most productive way possible". My head and my heart say a loud amen to that last sentence.

Chapter 5 - Gay Culture and Lifestyle

Out of the Shadows

Gay people have become much more visible than they used to be. They were always there in the shadows. They were people we knew but we didn't recognise that part of them. They have become visible not just through their angry protests and lobbying, but also because of a distinctive culture and lifestyle.

It's a mistake, however, to judge all gay people by it. Many choose to remain in the shadows, for a variety of reasons. They are not anxious to advertise themselves. There are others who are open about their sexual identity but choose to be low-key and don't want to be part of 'the scene'. Some have no obvious gay traits anyway and are conservative in their tastes. But many more gay people can be seen and want to be seen, than used to be the case.

Anne Robinson, in a recent *"Weakest Link"*, asked one of contestants if he was gay because he sported a neat moustache and a fashionable short haircut. Those features plus blue jeans, boots and a white snug-fitting T-shirt have been one common version of the 'gay look'.

I had a young man in one of my congregations who had problems that I was never able to diagnose. In despair he left the church. Some time later I met him at a wedding. I understood immediately what the issue was. He had finally 'come out' and adopted the look, had become fashionable in a low key way and was obviously paying a lot of attention to grooming, previously uncharacteristic of him.

Yes, a lot of gay men are narcissists, spending a lot of money on their appearance. The retail people talk a lot these days about the power of the pink pound. The tourist industry in Cape Town, where I now live, is very conscious of the pink Rand. There are other versions of the right look, involving a fair amount of leather as well as regular visits to the gym. Appearing 'butch' is a partially unconscious way of making up for being bullied and called 'sissy', or one of a variety of other derogatory names, at school. I admit that regular visits to the gym are one of the ways I try and compensate for my poor image of myself physically.

Most of this is an acquired life-style as a means of fighting back at the way society has forced gays to be incognito in the past, and as a statement of identity with the gay community. Gays have often been extremely lonely people and have not felt they belonged to any community. They didn't fit in at school or at home. They were often no good at sport and were not acceptable in some churches. Gay bars and clubs used to be illegal, and even after that changed they were often hidden up back alleys, had no windows and a heavily guarded door. It took more courage than many folk could muster to go in.

Whatever the rights and wrongs of gay activities, no group of people can go through life successfully with the kind of low self-esteem this kind of scenario created. The emergence of an identifiable gay community, therefore, with its own 'villages', bars, restaurants, shops, gyms and even gay travel agents who booked you on a Gay cruise, a holiday in Ibiza, or even a trip to the World Gay Games (the gay version of the Olympics !) was liberating for many gay people. There was somewhere they belonged and could leave their imprint.

Young people in particular need somewhere to 'hang out'. A

while ago I was staying with a minister friend in central London. On a sunny Saturday evening I strolled around the West End, including down Old Compton Street, Soho, the heart of London's gay ghetto. Crowds of young gay men overflowed from the pubs, enjoying the camaraderie of a pint together like straight young men were also doing in other streets and pubs. I walked past. But I wanted to join them. I've rarely felt I really belonged among crowds of macho straight males whether in a pub or a football match. I always felt I was the odd one out who might just be identified as different and get one of those 'looks', or possibly a hurtful remark. It's happened many times, though sometimes only in my imagination.

Gay Pride

Gay Pride festivals, one of the more offensive expressions of gay culture, especially to Christians, are in themselves a declaration of the sense of self-worth and identity that all of us need to have. They represent gay people kicking-back at all the kicking they feel they have received over the centuries and years.

The best known gay protester in England, Peter Tatchell, and his movement "Outrage" exemplify the kind of anger gay people still feel about their treatment. Tatchell has a bad image with many. But I have come to recognise that he is a very decent man who pays a heavy price to make people feel the pain that gay people feel. Physical gay-bashing is still common enough for gay people to have to watch where they walk at night. The awful case of Matthew Shepherd in the US, who was stalked by two small town homophobes, almost beaten to death and then left to die tied by barbed-wire to a fence, shocked America. A movie was made of the story.

Discrimination is still common in spite of laws against it, as evidenced by a Scottish hotelier who refused a double-room to two gay men. I do not deny that gay people sometimes provoke trouble by outrageous actions. I do not defend everything about the gay lifestyle. I am simply saying that I understand why things are as they are, and straight people need to recognise that much of it is a reaction to what straight people have done to gay people in the past.

Michael Vasey quotes the American Bishop William Swing as saying, "We have a homosexual ghetto as a monument to families all over the USA who cannot deal with their homosexual children". My experience is that a good proportion of those children are from evangelical homes, where the inability of parents to understand or accept their gay teenage children not only drives them away from home but also away from God.

Vasey emphasises my point about loneliness when he goes on, "Gay people differ from other cultural minorities in that they start out on their journey alone. In a society which has no positive or overt understanding of same-sex sexual attraction, the journey starts in unnamed darkness and involves considerable pain. Finding the space for self-exploration, never mind acceptance, involves emotionally isolated young people in one of two drastic strategies. The first is the construction of a divided personal identity; I conform to an expected stereotype and secretly establish an alternative being. The second is a more open self-revelation which often precipitates expulsion from the family, rejection by 'normal' society, and violence.... Before a person with homosexual tendencies can think through the issues that homosexuality raises, they have usually had to formulate a strategy for survival. This involves the discovery or creation of social space in which to be themselves".

Fifteen years ago I was not a teenager, but middle-aged, but I had to do just that. There was no way I could discover myself properly, and work through the implications, in a city and community where many people were observing me critically and one wrong move would be pounced on. Even those who were sympathetic were waiting for an opportunity to try and cure me, when I still did not know what exactly I was suffering from that needed to be cured.

So I went to live in another country in a gay ghetto, in a city with a large gay population. I even bought a condo on the beach - the epitome of gay lifestyle. The Pacific Ocean shimmering in the Californian sun, golden beaches, palm trees and hundreds of young people cruising down the beach track on their rollerblades. It was a very congenial place for healing and discovering myself. There was no one to reject me or make me feel odd. A lot of healing did take place there.

Gay Community

John McNeill writes of how important it has been for gay people to build a community where they can find support and security. "Gays in New York City, for example, have established the Lesbian and Gay Community Services Centre, a home that serves all members of the gay community. They have created SAGE (Senior Action in a Gay Environment) to help meet the needs of the older members. They have founded the Hetrick-Martin Institute for Gay Youth to help meet the social, medical, legal, and counselling needs of young gay people, which in turn brought into existence Harvey Milk High School (Milk was a gay mayor of San Francisco) for those students who could not survive and grow in the public school system. GMHC (the Gay Men's Health Crisis) has done a remarkable job of organising to meet the critical health needs of the Gay community, and of other groups as well, during the AIDS crisis. Many other excellent volunteer groups such as Persons with AIDS Coalition and the AIDS Resource Centre are striving to meet the needs of people with AIDS, gay and straight, to the best of their ability... There are hundreds of other organisations designed to meet the needs of gay people, among them the gay religious groups such as Dignity (for Catholics) Integrity (for Anglicans), Metropolitan Community Church, the Gay Synagogue, Lutherans Concerned, Affirmation, and many, many others. There are also innumerable social groups, political groups, and artistic groups. Lesbians and gay men have formed a very real community of love, concern and compassion".

Throughout history there have been clear evidences of people who were homosexual, and who were out, and expressed themselves in some form of community life, from the city of Sodom to the cities of ancient Greece. There were well-known figures who were homosexual, such as Alexander the Great. But there is a huge difference in how homosexuality was practised and expressed then as compared with today.

Michael Vasey traces the emergence of the present-day scene back to the late seventeenth century and the emergence of two male stereotypes in English society, the rake and the fop. The rake was the image of "lawless, assertive masculinity...he had sex with women and boys, indiscriminately". The fop, by contrast, was regarded as effeminate but in fact only had sex with women. To some extent this reflected ancient Greece rather than anticipated the twentieth century. The male performing the sexual acts, as opposed to the recipient, was frequently a married man.

It is impossible to know at this stage of history what proportion of them were genuinely gay and their marriages were a matter of social convenience, and what proportion were men who got their sex from boys because there were less problems than getting it from women, especially with the lack of modern contraceptives. The recipient was often a willing, or coerced, servant or male prostitute. Again it is impossible to know what proportion were homosexual by orientation.

Vasey says that it was in the 1680's that a new model emerged, the 'beau' who reflected more the elegance of the fop but in his sexual preference for boys, as well as women, reflected the rake. All this, of course, was in the context of married family life, particularly amongst the upper classes. The unmarried homosexual was much less common than today. The following century saw a reaction from this and there emerged a family life pattern which reigned until the latter part of the twentieth century; a pattern in which the homosexual community became separate and distinct.

It would be interesting to know what part the Wesleyan Revival of the eighteenth century played in this. It did affect the social structure of England considerably, even to the point of dragging the country from the edge of a bloody revolution like that which took place in France, according to the historian W.E. Lecky. Undoubtedly the British Isles today need a spiritual Revival. Such an extensive movement of the Holy Spirit would affect the gay community, as well as all other sections of society. But if my understanding of homosexuality is correct, gay people and their needs would still exist, and churches would still need to review how they handle, accommodate and welcome gay people. One hopes that Spiritual Revival would both curb gay excesses and create churches that are more truly loving and accepting.

Victorian Masculinity

The 19th century, brought the Industrial Revolution, the expansion of the British Empire and with it a great expansion in trade and economic prosperity. It also created the modern male, severely masculine and competitive. Until the emergence of the feminist movement in the twentieth century women were marginalised. Economic life and expansion was everything, and women were excluded from that. But so were other aspects of human reality. "Love, desire, beauty, poetry - were relegated to the margins of serious life" (Vasey).

The home became the refuge from the rigours of the market place, so strengthening what has become the modern nuclear family unit. There was little place in this economic structure for the softness or artistry of the gay man, and little likelihood of his acceptance into family life. The competitiveness of business life in particular was not conducive to the kind of male bonding experienced in earlier centuries, adding yet further to the isolation of any with homosexual tendencies.

So homosexual activity moved to the fringes of society, into darkness, seclusion and separation. Homosexuals were seen as people of the shadows with strange and evil ways. This has some comparison with Christians in the first century.   The authorities of the Roman Empire suspected and accused them of all kinds of evil (including cannibalism because they 'ate the body and blood of Jesus', and atheism because they had no gods you could touch and handle) because they were such a distinctly separate society.   The Victorians had a passion for legislating against evil deeds, which was perhaps one of the less attractive results of the Second Evangelical Awakening. This, together with the changes and trends described, brought about the situation in which gays found themselves until very recent years; a group not only despised and isolated but guilty of serious crimes.

Stonewall Inn

The event which gay people celebrate, as marking the turning-point, was a riot that took place at the Stonewall Inn in New York in 1969. It's regarded as marking the birth of the modern gay movement. The inn was in the heart of what is now regarded as the gay village, the area of south Manhattan around Christopher Street.

I was in that area, possibly even in the Stonewall Inn, three years before then. It was my first trip to the US. I was doing an exchange with a Baptist pastor from Pittsburg.   He had arranged for me to be hosted while passing through New York by another Baptist pastor. From the moment he met me at Idlewild airport, later to become Kennedy, I was puzzled. He certainly didn't fit the Baptist pastor mould, and was wary of me. He introduced me to a friend in whose apartment we would be staying. The three of us went out for dinner around midnight in a part of Manhattan, and in a restaurant, where I felt distinctly uncomfortable. It was only when later they climbed into bed together that the alarm bells started ringing. I was sharing the same room. I was near petrified!

In 1969 repeated police raids on the Stonewall Inn drove to

their limit the despised assortment of folk who made the Inn their refuge. Gay descriptions of the event put a lot of emphasis on a mixture of gays and drag-queens, provoked not only by police harassment, but by anxiety about the terminal sickness of Judy Garland in a nearby hospital. Judy was a gay icon, very much as Barbara Streisand has been in more recent decades. Gay folk love their show-biz icons, and they don't have to be gay.

For a long time they had accepted the raids fairly passively. The average gay boy is hardly a match for a New York cop! But on that particular night all the resentment, anger, hurt boiled over. Legend describes drag queens attacking the cops with their stiletto heels and anything they could use as a weapon. Whatever, it was a turning-point. Gays decided to stand up and fight, by whatever means they could; usually protest demonstrations and any political means open to them.

In Britain Stonewall is the name of a well-known and well established organisation that works for gay rights through political means. Gay Pride marches were one of the first expressions of this new found militancy. In more recent years they have put more emphasis on celebration. The world's largest, in Sydney Australia, is called a Mardi Gras, like the well-known carnivals in Rio or New Orleans. But initially the emphasis was on protest and demands for political rights.

Very large numbers attend the events in cities like New York, San Francisco, Los Angeles, London, as well as Sydney. They have been, and still are, a very important part in creating a sense of gay identity and community. Cape Town recently had its annual Pride events; one in the city centre and one in a black township, the latter possibly the first of its kind. For better or worse the gay community will never allow itself to be pushed back into the shadows; it is here to stay and the Church has to respond to what it is saying through more than negativity and condemnation.

Integrating Gay People into Society

Nothing will do more to lessen that sense of being a separate community, and some of the extremes that produces, than a fuller integration of gay people into the main-stream of society, including the churches. Even to those who are members, gay churches are a poor second best. Gay Christians do not want to produce a 'gay' version of the Christian faith. Gay churches, with their oddities and sometimes fractiousness, only exist because of the inability of conservative Christians to make space for their gay brothers and sisters. Behind all the anger and counter-culture there is a cry amongst gay people to belong, to be accepted.

Michael Vasey suggests that one of the reasons evangelical Christians resist decisive change in attitudes to gay people is because Christians are also struggling for identity in an unsympathetic world. They are also a counter-culture. In Britain, and Europe in general, even to use the 'god' word, except in swearing, is to make yourself a social misfit. There is embarrassment and almost imperceptibly a space emerges that puts you on the edge of any circle of people you are with. So Christians lose the warmth of acceptance that they also are craving for. In Europe Christians are becoming a small minority seeking to preserve their culture and survive. Evangelical ministers sometimes try to strengthen the identity of their flocks, and give them a sense of security, by telling them what 'they are not' as well as what 'they are'. And one of the worst manifestations of the world of which 'they are not a part' is homosexuality. No wonder straight evangelicals don't wish to be seen as accommodating to gays.

Acquired and Innate Culture

At this point I want to make a distinction between what I will call 'Acquired Culture' and 'Innate Culture'. Many of the things mentioned so far are those which Christians find most repugnant. Gay Pride parades often give the impression that gay people are freaks with no sense of shame. Gay protests, at discrimination against them, often go over the top. I've identified the extremes as being, in part, a reaction to homophobia. I've also described them as being a cry for identity and a sense of community.

Last week a Christian woman described to me a gay man at her place of work. He had shared his difficulty in accepting himself as well as being accepted. She had sympathised with much of what he said, and affirmed him as a person. "But" she said "when he began to accept himself more he turned into somebody else. He started to wear tight jeans and T-shirts, showy belt-buckles, and adopt some of the mannerisms". For some gay men this is a mark of 'coming out', a celebration of a rite of passage, an identification with a people and its culture. For other gay men it's just silly, and for some repugnant, as the woman found it. It is, in part, an 'acquired culture'.

But there are other characteristics which seem to be an inherent part of being gay. They are true of the majority of gay people and may evidence themselves even when a person is in denial or in the closet. They can be repressed to an extent but have a way of manifesting themselves unconsciously. They reflect something deeper in the person that cannot easily be altered. I will not attempt to explain it in terms of genetics or chromosomes. I would be out of my depth.

All I can say is that they are part of 'me', part of my personality and it's very difficult to conceive of them not being there. Most of the time I live outwardly like a straight person in a straight world. But a good deal of the time I have to repress myself, in order to be accepted in the straight community, particularly the evangelical community. It is as automatic for me to admire a good-looking guy, who I pass in the street, as for a heterosexual to admire the opposite sex. I turn my head instinctively. Sometimes I give myself away in doing it and so have to be extra careful.

A straight person will often make a comment, to any friend he is with, about a person he noticed; "Wow did you see her!" I can make comments to a few of my straight friends. But most of the time they are a bit embarrassed, even though they accept me for who I am. I can also be a bit 'camp'. When I was a student doing teacher training I brought the house down, during a college concert, by a camp impersonation I did. I was so popular for weeks that I got elected to the Student Representative Council on the strength of it.

Camp

I'm probably unconsciously camp at times and it gives me away. My taste in clothes, music, art, books and in house decoration, definitely reflect something of my more feminine or gay side. A woman I know, and who I met a few days ago in a shopping mall, noticed amongst my purchases a Maeve Binchy novel. For a second she looked puzzled and said, "Aren't they a woman thing?" I had hardly thought about it. I buy them because I enjoy them. I've done too much repressing of the real me in my life. These things have nothing to do with morality.

When I moved to Cape Town in 1976 I remember furnishing my bedroom in a fairly severe style because I thought it would look more masculine. Some years later I built my first home. I designed it myself. It was my dream house, where I expected to spend the rest of my life. I chose every piece of wood, every fitting, every decoration or piece of furniture. It was so much 'my' house reflecting who I am that I didn't hold back. The lounge carpet was a soft pink and the easy chair coverings had pink roses. All the china decorations, displayed on specially built shelves, were very non-masculine. A close minister colleague, viewing it for the first time, had a very puzzled look on his face as he tried to work it out.

Around that time friends who I visited in Switzerland gave me a beautiful stuffed toy lion, at a time when I was feeling sad. It was the first in a small collection of stuffed animals I've built up, each representing a different place in which I've lived. It's not a characteristic of all gay men but it certainly is a feature of Gay culture. While ministering to gay men dying of AIDS I found that it was very common for them to have their favourite stuffed toy animal with them.

Some of the time I need to be with gay people, just as men need to be with men, women with women, young people to be with young people, old people with other oldies, expat Brits with other expat Brits, no doubt - blind or handicapped people with other similarly disadvantaged. In these situations we experience an empathy we all need, and miss for much of the time. I enjoy the campness, the distinctly gay humour and jokes. I enjoy the amazing artistry amongst gay people. Where would the world be without so many famous artists and actors who were, and are, Gay? Their number is legion.

The same is true in the world of music - serious and pop. In the movie *Doing Time on Maple Drive* a gay twenty-year old comes out to his best friend. The friend struggles a bit and asks what difference it's going to make to their relationship. The gay guy promises that his friend won't have to like musicals, and that he won't sing songs from the shows when they go on trips together. I have vivid memories of a trip I made to Austria with a few American gay friends. We did the tour of the places associated with "The Sound of Music". I can still see the look on the face of our young tour guide as we bellowed out "The hills are alive", "Do- re-me" and all the other favourites.

I enjoy Abba, especially singing "Dancing Queen" and the Weather Girls singing "It's raining men", which gay men love to dance to. At the present time the "Scissors Sisters" are beginning to hit the pop charts and I hear their song "I don't feel like dancing" playing at the gym, supermarkets and on a very popular TV soap. I've twice asked the teenage children of evangelical minister friends what they think of the group and the song. Enthusiastic approval both times. But most of the group are gay men and the culture of their music is distinctly gay. But regardless of some negative things about the group, that song is fun and great to dance to, even if only in your bedroom.

Can Christians have Fun?

Why is it so difficult for some Christians to let their hair down and have fun? No one can read some of the Old Testament, Psalm 104 for instance, or some of the parables of Jesus, and not believe that God has fun. Gay people know how to have fun, and I like that. I enjoy wearing the kind of T-shirts and tank-tops a 16 year old might also wear. I love going around trendy clothes shops with other gay men, trying things on. Not many straight men enjoy shopping of that kind.

There is an immature side of me, that comes from being gay, even though Christian leaders and friends often tell me how 'wise' I am when counselling, and how well respected I am as a preacher and teacher. I like kicking stones when I walk down a country road. I sometimes run down the street, or walk on top of a wall, for no other reason than the fun of doing it. There is so much of life in which I have to act very responsibly and with maturity.

We all need the times when we give ourselves permission to be childlike again. Jesus made a great deal of how we need to be like children in order to enter the Kingdom of God and its blessings. One of the great problems for the modern male is that he is a loner, afraid of opening himself up, afraid of touch or manifesting weakness. It's a huge social problem and has become worse through the advent of the more militant kind of feminism. It's a characteristic that gay men, for the most part, do not share. Why would I want to reject that part of being gay, in the name of rejecting a bad lifestyle?

There are many positive and good things about Gay culture and lifestyle. The story of the AIDS struggle, particularly in the days when it was seen as a gay plague, is a story that features immense compassion, even heroism. Some of the most emotional and meaningful times of my life have been those

AIDS memorial services where there was a sense of community closeness rarely experienced elsewhere.

I enjoy the bizarre situations that can arise when gay men and lesbians are in community, and it's the women who have their heads under the car bonnet and fixing the roof, while the guys bake the cakes. It was amazing to sing in a gay choir in California, where there was always a shortage of female sopranos and male basses, while there were women who could sing the male parts and one or two guys who sang alto. In straight choirs there is nearly always a shortage of altos and tenors. How do we explain that, if homosexuality is not in part, at least, nature?

My straight readers may even be embarrassed by some of the things I've admitted and wonder why I expose myself to ridicule by writing of them. I am not embarrassed because it represents part of who I am, as well as what I've had to struggle with because of the opinions of society. These characteristics I've described as innate are common to gay people. But in a sense they are no different from things that make the Welsh what they are and different from the Scots, or Italians or Africans.

Innate Culture

In recent years I have worked with students in Port Elizabeth, in the Eastern Cape. Even though these are post-apartheid days and those of student age don't suffer from the hang-ups of the past, it is still not easy building racially integrated student organisations. The problem is cultural not racial. One characteristic of African people which I enjoy tremendously is their innate sense of rhythm and dance. I have never come across an African who does not have it, though there must be some. Old mamas waiting at a bus stop, after a day of doing domestic work, dance while they wait. Serious political meetings often erupt into dancing.

I once preached at a black church where the missionary society that planted the church didn't approve of dancing. So there was no place for it in the liturgy. But when that part of the service was over, they sang a 'going-home' song, accompanied by a line dance. But this love of dancing often causes a problem in racially-integrated social or religious occasions. Many white people simply have no sense of rhythm, can't dance and are far too embarrassed to try. These differences are not just culturally imposed. There is something innate about them. People can learn to adjust to the ways of other ethnic and cultural groups. But there are times when they need to be with those who share the same culture, so they have freedom to be fully themselves. Only a small proportion of my life is spent with gay people, but I need those times.

When it comes to acquired characteristics there is a much greater variety of practice, just as in the straight community. The young gay men and women who spend their time in bars, take drugs, are promiscuous, have more in common with straight young people who do similar things than they do with the large number of gay people who do not spend their time in bars, take drugs or are sexually promiscuous.

It's a caricature of gays which suggests that in these aspects of life-style they are fundamentally worse than straight folk. Our newspapers are full of stories of prominent people who have had extra-marital affairs and they are not gay. Much of gay culture is a result of the Fall, and all of it is affected by the Fall, as is heterosexual culture.

Double Standards

Many evangelical churches, in my opinion, are guilty of double standards. On the one hand they are failing to grapple with the rising tide of immorality and promiscuity amongst their own members. There is no question that the much later age at which people are getting married, is creating serious problems. Parents, even Christian parents, encourage the pursuit of career at the expense of marriage.

It's my suspicion that if the average Evangelical church pastor knew the proportion of his young people who are not celibate, he would get a severe shock. Probably it's a relief not to know, because we wouldn't know how to deal with it. Where we become aware of people who've overstepped the line, we have difficulty taking strong action just because we know how many others there must be. We don't want to be guilty of treating folk unfairly.

But when it comes to gay people in the fellowship, few are going to protest if we take a strong line; so they either toe the line or they are 'out' regardless of what it does to them emotionally and spiritually. There are many things about gay life-style and culture which are very wrong, but gay people are entitled to understanding, fairness and justice like anyone else.

Chapter Six - "What does the Bible say?"

The $64,000 Question

For me, and for most evangelicals, this is the biggie question. Evangelicals hold a high view of Scripture. We believe that the Bible is infallible as originally given. It comes to us as the Word of God. It is our guide in all matters of faith and conduct. I subscribe fully to that view. For more than forty years I have been known as an expository preacher and teacher who seeks to interpret the Bible accurately. I see any deviation from a thoroughly evangelical view of Scripture as the beginning of a slippery slope in Christian theology.

So I find it hard to write this chapter because the last thing I want is to appear speculative in my handling of Scripture. Having said that I believe we all have a responsibility to be open to fresh understanding of Scripture. I wrote earlier of that being a prime Reformation principle. As an evangelical Christian, who also believes in the Holy Spirit, I believe that Word and Spirit stand together. "All Scripture is given by inspiration of God (God-breathed NIV)" (2 Timothy 3:16). That inspiration comes from and through the Holy Spirit, who is the Breath of God. So as a faithful student of the Word I have to be willing to re-examine my own understanding of the Bible, and also the understanding of others.

The Church's understanding of Scripture is not a static thing. The Holy Spirit is constantly at work renewing our minds, clarifying our understanding, and sometimes changing it. 2

Timothy 3:16 goes on to say "and is useful for teaching, rebuking, correcting...". The Holy Spirit may even use the correcting word to correct our understanding of what the Word says. We have to be aware of the danger of believing in the infallibility of our own understanding of the infallible book. All of us come to the Bible with pre-conceptions and prejudices that shape our interpretation and determine answers. I must resist any temptation I may have as a gay person to try and make the Bible say what I might want it to say. We must also be prepared to live with unanswered questions. The strong desire to have clear answers often drives us to oversimplification of very complex issues.

So my purpose is not to try and explain away what the Bible says, or pretend that the Bible does not condemn what is referred to as 'homosexual' acts or offenders. My purpose is to persuade evangelicals to ask again what the Bible means when it condemns homosexuality, and in particular what it means for today.

Most of us have treated the teaching of the Bible on this subject as an open and shut case. To query the traditional understanding of Scripture is seen as an attempt to undermine or denigrate the message of the Bible itself. That query means to forfeit the right to be regarded as an orthodox Christian. Even some Christians who are gay, including some practising ones, accept that viewpoint. I've referred earlier to a lesbian, from a very conservative Christian home, who walked out of my office convinced that she was damned even though I was convinced, and tried to convince her, that she was a true child of God, who might be straying but was not rejected.

I feel a great sadness at the number of Christian people, who are gay, who leave the Church because they've been convinced it is not possible to be gay and a Christian. I grow very weary at times trying to persuade them otherwise.

The Importance of Context

It does scant justice to the Bible to establish a fixed position, which has far reaching consequences for many people, on half a dozen proof texts the interpretation of which is at least questionable.

It is not enough to ask "What does the Bible say about homosexuality?" We need to ask also *"What do the verses concerned mean in their context, what are they referring to ? Is what they are referring to the same as what we are referring to when we use those verses for guidance today? Is the cultural context comparable?"*

The Pharisees were often guilty of an unspiritual and unintelligent application of Old Testament law, which did an immense amount of harm and was condemned by Jesus. One test of whether our understanding of Scripture is valid is to ask "Does our interpretation make sense? Does it fit the facts as we find them?" It is not the only test but it's an important one.

Scholars operating on what appear to be sound exegetical principles sometimes come up with interpretations that leave you feeling "there's something not quite right here". Much recent writing on homosexuality leaves me with that feeling. There has been some re-examination of the Scripture texts and issues related to them, but most evangelical writers come up with essentially the same answers, answers that change nothing for those who are most affected and continue to suffer.

If they have come up with those answers because they are genuinely convinced that no other understanding is possible, then I respect that position. But I am not convinced that is the whole picture. In chapter three I dealt with the factors that make evangelicals resistant to the possibility of change. I have also pointed out how evangelicals, as a body, have changed their opinions on a number of other important issues in recent decades, because their understanding of Scripture changed.

There has been major development in our understanding of the Person and Work of the Holy Spirit. For years I wrestled with the question, "What is the baptism in the Holy Spirit? Is baptism a term that can only be applied to what happened at Pentecost, or is it a term that can be used of outpourings of the Holy Spirit on individuals today? Should we seek and ask for such an experience?"

For me the question was a profoundly practical one. I was not satisfied with the results of years of preaching a traditional evangelical viewpoint. There was something lacking in the lives of the people I pastored, as well as my own life. There had to be something 'more'. But before I could deal with the practical problem I had to deal with the theological problem, because my Reformed Evangelical background said that the 'baptism in the Holy Spirit' was something that took place at conversion, and only then, and that to say otherwise was theologically unsound and experientially dangerous. I read just about everything I could lay my hands on, looking at both sides of the argument. The arguments on interpretation of Scripture, from equally evangelical, equally scholarly, equally spiritual, writers seemed to cancel each other out. Both could make a very good case for their point of view and both were convinced that their interpretation was the correct one.

I was in near despair; it began to immobilise me in my ministry. Then one day I listened to a taped sermon by David Pawson in which he listed all the different understandings of the term "baptism in the Holy Spirit". But then he asked the very simple question, *"Which one works?"* That clinched it for me. If a doctrine or teaching is true, it will be evidenced in practice.

I had already discovered that when people received specific prayer and ministry for an outpouring, or baptism, in the Spirit - something dynamic did happen, even if it was sometimes delayed, and in most cases it transformed the lives of those concerned. Arriving at a clear conviction on that transformed my own ministry and my church. The proof of the pudding was in the eating. I discovered that even using the term 'baptism' rather than 'fullness', or some other term more acceptable to traditional evangelicals seemed to make a difference. It is a matter of honouring the Holy Spirit and his work. Over more recent years evangelicals have reached a broad consensus on that subject which embraces good theology and good experience.

We need a Consensus

It is important for me that we reach that kind of consensus on the subject of homosexuality, an understanding which is faithful to Scripture but makes sense of human experience and need as we find it. An unworkable sexual ethic, unworkable usually because it's unbiblical, can only lead to more of what it is seeking to avoid. God is the source of all true knowledge. A right understanding of Bible teaching, therefore, will find harmony with what we learn from other disciplines, science, medicine, psychology and sociology. The fact that traditional evangelical teaching, on what the Bible says about homosexuality, doesn't fit the facts as we find them today, and often has serious repercussions in the physical, psychological and spiritual lives of gay people, makes me feel that there has to be a fresh appraisal. *Something is wrong somewhere.*

In more recent years some evangelical scholars and writers have recognised the weakness of building arguments on a number of proof texts, the interpretation of some of which is far from clear. They have attempted to take a bigger picture and concentrate their attention more on Genesis 1 and 2, the creation of male and female and the marriage ordinance. But that doesn't help in our quest for how we deal with homosexuality today. Genesis 1 and 2 deal with life before the Fall. The Fall profoundly changed everything. It's been a cleaning up operation ever since. And often we make an even bigger mess.

God's salvation work, in its end-time totality, is the only thing that arrests the decline. We cannot make rules for governing society, or even the church, as if there had been no Fall. That leads to the error of 'perfectionism'. And Scripture doesn't always give us exact answers as to how we clear up the mess. Sometimes it just leaves us with unanswered questions.

For example, does Genesis 1:28 allow for birth control to be practised? What happens when man has 'filled the earth' and there is overpopulation as in some parts of the world today? As the purpose of the sex act appears to be procreation, is oral sex legitimate? Is masturbation legitimate and in what circumstances?

In these areas evangelical Christians have sometimes been guilty of double standards. The 'official' line is often very different from the reality of what happens. Masturbation can sometimes prevent worse things happening. So people work it out for themselves regardless of what the official line may be. But many evangelical Christians require homosexuals to be celibate, and condemn the practice of masturbation, without giving any serious guidance as to how natural sexual urges are to be channelled.

Living in a Fallen world leaves us with difficult choices, because sometimes circumstances force us to choose between lesser evils. The ideal is not always a present possibility. Putting the hurdle too high can lead to despair and abandonment of all attempts to improve. We grapple with the same kind of problems when it comes to marital breakdowns. The issues are not simple and Scripture does not always give us clear guidance.

Polygamy & Divorce

Homosexuality is one of the most difficult of these issues, but not the only one. If Genesis 1-2 do give us a clear pattern for all time, a pattern exemplified in the nuclear family unit of western world Christians, why did polygamy appear on the Biblical scene so quickly? Monogamy is implicit in the story of

Adam and Eve, since God created only one wife for Adam. Yet polygamy is adopted from the time of Lamech (Genesis 4:19). It was practised by such great men of the Faith as Abraham, Gideon, David and Solomon. Sin resulted from it in some cases, but polygamy as such is not condemned in the Old Testament.

There is no word for 'bachelor' in the Hebrew of the Old Testament. There is no recognition in the creation accounts that some might be called to singleness. It is only in the New Testament that such a concept appears, and it is this that gives a pattern for the teaching of celibacy, acknowledging the fact that the Genesis 1-2 pattern of family life is not always possible. Lacking clear Scripture answers, deductions have to be made and different patterns established that cannot claim to be built on Genesis 1-2.

There are other areas where we see how difficult it is to build present day practice on Old Testament instructions and commands. Many of the instructions are there precisely because the world is Fallen, and they are an accommodation to the realities of it. We will come to the specific issue of Leviticus 18:22 and 20:13, which deal with homosexuality, later. But there are other results of the Fall which are dealt with in a way we would now regard as sub-Christian, particularly the role of the woman in marriage. These commands are seen by the New Testament as an accommodation.

Mark 10:2-12; Matthew 19:3-12 and Luke 16:14-18 give us one example of this. The Pharisees raise the question of divorce with Jesus and quote Old Testament instructions (in Deuteronomy 24:1-4) that if a man becomes displeased with his wife, over some kind of 'indecency', he may get rid of her provided he writes her a certificate of divorce. "Indecency" had come to have a very wide meaning; even burning her husband's porridge, raising her voice or gossiping in the street were regarded as sufficient reasons.

Jesus tells them that divorce was never God's plan and refers them to Genesis 1:27 and 2:24. The Mosaic instruction, which the Pharisees had evidently turned into permanent permission for divorce, existed only because of the hardness of men's heart as a result of sin (Mark 10:5). It was given to alleviate some of the cruelty women experienced as a result of the Fall. The certificate was given to protect her. She could have been stoned to death if suspected of adultery.

Jesus makes clear that the Old Testament instructions were given at a particular time for a particular purpose, an aspect of a lot of other legislation in the first five books of the Bible not to be overlooked. Quite apart from the issue of divorce, Mosaic legislation reflects an attitude to women clearly not intended at Creation. There is an implied contempt for women. Wives were disposable adjuncts to male life. No instructions were given for a situation where a woman was displeased with her husband. There is a latent cruelty to women in the whole picture, even though Moses sought to limit it. There is none of the partnership between male and female that we see in Genesis 1:27 and 2:18, 20- 24.

The Treatment of Women

There is a clear warning here about lifting Biblical instructions out of their context and applying them to the present day. While evangelical Christians are rightly negative about some of the extremes of radical feminism, we cannot deny that women have frequently been treated as inferiors, and in some places they still are, especially in Africa where I live, and in most Muslim countries. That treatment has come about through a mind-set that men have developed as a result of the Fall.

Most evangelicals believe that the male was created to take the initiative and created with characteristics and abilities that enable him to protect and care for his family. But there is no question that those good characteristics have sometimes turned to bad, to the severe detriment of women. The macho aspect of male culture reflects the Fall more than it does Creation. It is this, in part, which has led to much of the cruelty inflicted on people who don't fit that image, particularly gay men. In my experience women have fewer problems with homosexuality than men do.

There is no question that Genesis 1 and 2 are fundamental in establishing a foundation and pattern for human life. That pattern sees marriage between a man and a woman as the norm for all. But that pattern was established in the context of an ideal society. The Fall had not yet taken place. It doesn't conceive of people who are not in a heterosexual marriage relationship. It gives no instructions or help for those who do not marry. Yet Jesus did not marry, nor did the greatest of the Apostles, Paul. Paul in fact recommends singleness as being the better state (1 Corinthians 7:25ff). But that also is not intended to be taken out of context and applied generally. It was advice for a particular time and a particular place and for a particular purpose. The ideal of Genesis 1-2 will always be there and remains foundational, but historical and cultural circumstances do bring other factors into play, for which we have to find answers.

The Traditional verses

It is not my purpose in the scope of this book to deal exhaustively with the particular texts which refer to homosexuality. That would require a book in itself. A good many books that have been written do that, and do it better than I could. The majority of those from evangelical sources take the traditional point of view. "Revisionist" approaches to the subject, revisionist being the term evangelicals sometimes use of opposing views, come by and large from more liberal theological sources. Some of the best of those writings are very helpful in showing that there are good grounds for questioning traditionalist reasoning. But some of the answers they give will not satisfy those committed to a conservative view of Scripture, including me. Michael Vasey in his book *"Strangers and Friends"* has produced a scholarly, closely argued work from an evangelical point of view. It is one of the few books from a conservative source, and from a theologian, that challenges traditional arguments. But it is not an easy book for the layman to understand.

My first purpose is to make a number of general points about where I am coming from, and the things that influence my thinking when approaching the Biblical texts. Then I want to take a more detailed look at those verses. I will suggest there have been serious faults in traditional approaches and interpretation. Thirdly, I want to bring into the picture some other verses of Scripture that don't seem to get discussed.

We don't Play Games with the Bible

So, I want to make clear first where I am coming from and where I am seeking to go. I don't plan to present my own 'revisionist' understanding of the relevant Scriptures and try and turn the traditional arguments on their head, so that the Bible becomes a 'gay-friendly' book. I wish it was.

But I have to be honest, as well as faithful. Good Christians don't play games with the Bible. I do think it's disgraceful the way Christians have used the Bible to beat gay people around the head. I believe it is very wrong to go on using the Bible texts in the way they've been used for centuries, refusing to take cognisance of how much better we now understand homosexuality. And, that better understanding does make a great deal of difference as to how we understand what the Bible says, and how we apply it.

But there are warnings in Scripture which can't just be explained away, and gay people need to take them seriously. That doesn't mean that those warnings are written in 'red letters' which make them more serious than other warnings about sin in the Bible. The pastor of the church where I am a member, at the time of writing, has a very compassionate attitude towards gay people and is prepared to go a long way to bring about change. He has stuck his neck out on my behalf and has been criticised for doing so. To make sure he understood my position correctly, he asked me "Graham, if a Christian who was gay came to you, told you that he was in an active loving relationship with another Christian of the same sex, would you pat him on the head and say - don't worry, it's OK?" I answered in the negative. But I confess that when I've been faced with some situations like that I have found it very hard to give a firm answer. I ache for them and their dilemma and I make sure they know that. But I stop short of giving approval, because I believe that Scripture, as I understand it right now, doesn't allow me to go that far. I can't play games with the Bible.

Secondly, let me underline what I've already made clear. I believe homosexuality is a result of the Fall, and not part of God's creative purpose. Gay people love to talk about God's rainbow creation, of which being gay is one of many expressions. I understand that. It's very appealing and affirming if you are gay. Too many people try to make homosexuals feel they are freaks or specially wicked. Some of my friends and colleagues can't handle the fact that I am comfortable being who I am. But no person can function happily or successfully in life, including in serving God, unless he is comfortable with who he is.

For some people it settles the whole issue if you admit, as I am doing, that homosexuality is a deviation from God's creative purposes. In their estimation that implies it is sinful and therefore the homosexual is, in a particular sense, a sinner. It does *not* mean that. Jesus faced that issue with the man who was born blind and got healed (John 9). His disciples asked whose sin it was that caused the blindness, caused this departure from God's creative plan - was it his own sin or his parents? Jesus said it was neither. Blindness at birth may simply be a result of being born into a Fallen world, which in this case Jesus was going to reverse. Without the miracle performed by Jesus the man would have remained blind all his life.

Many blind people are permanently blind and no one suggests it is a result of their personal sin or lack of faith. There are many unfortunate results of the Fall that severely handicap people. But those suffering the results have to live their lives and do it in the most fulfilling way they can.

A couple of years ago I was standing in the departure lounge of Los Angeles airport when I noticed a smartly dressed lady dragging a suitcase by its strap, as many people do, except that she had the strap over her shoulder. She was less than three feet tall, not much higher than the suitcase. She was a well-proportioned dwarf. My first reaction was "There is no way I would show myself publicly like that if I had that disability". I was thinking of all the humiliation it would involve. She would probably need to be lifted on to the aircraft. But then I realised that whatever your disability in life may be, you cannot just stay at home. Life is to be lived. And this woman was doing just that with no obvious sign that she was embarrassed. Suddenly I felt admiration for her rather than pity.

In one particular sense the gay person is a disadvantaged human being, but one among many with varying disadvantages. In his or her case, it is the disadvantage of being unable to express love and have intimacy in the accepted heterosexual way. For some gay people, but only some, that is a burden and a matter of great sorrow.

Heterosexual Christians need to face up to that. It will not do to try and push gay people back into the closet and tell them to stop whinging. Gay people are here and there has to be some realistic answer to their need to have as fulfilling a life as possible. Some well-meaning heterosexuals sometimes try and give them that by surrounding them with a 'spiritual armed guard' protecting them from predators and temptation. I don't see that as the answer.

It is partly because Christians who are homosexual have remained in the closet so long, mainly out of fear, that their heterosexual brothers and sisters have been able to ignore their needs. Now they are faced with it they don't know to handle it. The changes in society are affecting the churches for good or bad. Increasingly I find the laity are willing to listen to what I have to say on this subject in a way their leaders are not, partly because the laity live in the real world more than the clergy do.

Approaching the Verses

I need now to make a few points about our approach to Scripture before turning to the relevant verses.

The first is that the Bible says less on the subject of homosexuality than people seem to imagine. There are seven texts normally used in the argument. One or two are indirect, as well as very brief references. The two in Leviticus are repeats of the same command. With the exception of chapters 18-19 of Genesis, all are brief and give very little clue as to their context and meaning. The only detailed account, that of Genesis, has little to say which can be applied directly to contemporary understanding or practice of homosexuality. It is the least convincing passage for a case against homosexuality as we know it.

Jesus makes no reference to homosexuality and there is no reference at all in the gospels. It is not mentioned directly by any of the non-Pauline letters; though Jude makes a reference to the 'perversion' in Sodom and Gomorrah. Yet it has become the subject of an enormously fierce debate and argument and threatens to split some sections of the Christian Church.

I suspect that this has more to do with wider issues than homosexuality itself. There is a tremendous battle going on for the soul of some denominations, the Church of England being an obvious case in point. Evangelicals are fighting hard to resist any further erosions of fundamental truth. I sympathise with that entirely. The ordination of homosexual clergy and bishops has become one part of that battle, but a part of it that gains the public's attention much more than debates about church structures or dogma.

As we know, such fights - though sometimes very necessary - often generate as much heat as light. In the process some negative things happen as well as the good things the contestants are seeking to achieve. Gay pressure groups like "Outrage" do not help by their disruption of church services in which they are intruders. So one of the results of these debates is a negative and exaggerated view of gay people as a whole. A closed mind develops towards homosexuals, not directly because of what they are or do, but because they have become part of a much bigger battle. Hence a few verses of Scripture take on enormous significance.

The second consideration, which is of great importance, is that the Bible passages concerned appear to have no concept of same-sex attraction being from nature and not nurture. Homosexuality is always understood in terms of choice, sexual acts and wicked perversion.

Bible scholars and teachers have always had to grapple with the question of the extent to which cultural context, and the limited knowledge of the period, influenced the Biblical writers. The problem of the coming together of the human and the divine affects a number of big issues. How could Jesus be fully man and yet also fully God? All sides of the Christian community have struggled with that one. Theological liberals have often stressed his humanity at the expense of his deity, evangelicals the opposite. How can Salvation be totally God's work and yet human beings be held responsible for their sin, and for not responding to the Gospel? Evangelicals are deeply divided on that issue because there are factors which defy all human logic.

The inspiration of Scripture is a further problem area. How can the Bible be fully inspired by God, and be written by real men who were writing in their own words, reflecting their own individuality, and each his particular background? That in itself could be a subject for a whole chapter. But a summary answer would be to say, that the writers were protected by the Holy Spirit from error, whilst at the same time reflecting their historical context and environment.

One of the marvels of the Bible is that it speaks in the kind of language which can be understood in every generation and every culture. This mean that on subjects like Creation, as an example, it does not use the kind of scientific language which would quickly become dated and need revision, but at the same time it is not unscientific. The Bible is primarily a book of Salvation, reflecting the background of each stage of Salvation history, but not entering into details which are not relevant.

We do not know if in the time of Moses, or even in the time of Paul, there was any concept of people who were homosexual by nature. The Jews believed there were people who were born 'eunuchs', and Jesus makes reference to them (Matthew 19:12), but it's unlikely the term included the concept of someone born homosexual. We are left guessing as to what the Biblical writers knew, and therefore to what extent the text, even though inspired by God, speaks into our present situation with clarity.

One of our problems, as evangelicals, is that it has always been assumed that the Bible speaks with 'clarity' on this issue. It is clearly not so. Until recent years there was only a limited understanding amongst ordinary people of homosexuality as an orientation rather than a lifestyle choice. In that situation it is understandable that direct application of the Biblical texts to present day practice would be made. *But once we understand that, for a considerable number of people, being homosexual is not a matter of choice, it makes a whole difference to our understanding and application of the Biblical texts.*

A third factor that should influence our thinking is that all the Biblical passages are about people who chose to do wicked acts, and usually in the context of false religion. The Leviticus texts are the only possible exception and even then there is a strong likelihood of influence from false religion. The New

Testament references are all in the context of wickedness and heathenism.

There is no concept of a citizen in good standing who happened to be homosexual by nature, and had a loving monogamous relationship with a partner. Even less is there any concept of a Christian, who was walking with God and seeking to serve God faithfully, being in that situation. But today there are many Christians in that situation and I've found it particularly true of lesbians. A small book I've found helpful in my researches is George Hopper's *"Reluctant Journey"*. An Evangelical layman and preacher, Hopper describes how for most of his life he held traditional evangelical prejudices against gay people. It was getting to know a group of gay Christians that changed his outlook and forced him to change his views.

Few straight Christians have taken the trouble, or even been willing, to fellowship with a group of gay Christians who really know Jesus and are filled with his Spirit. My first visit to a so-called gay church, which I described earlier, shook me because I sensed the Holy Spirit's presence so strongly. That simply doesn't fit in with the scenario painted in the Biblical passages, which should force us to ask whether the Biblical texts can be applied in the simplistic way we have applied them.

Most people who write on this issue see Romans 1 as being the clearest passage, because one is left with no doubt that same sex acts are Paul's subject for condemnation. In the symposium, *"The Way Forward"* Dr Rowan Williams, the present Archbishop of Canterbury, comments "What makes this text (Romans 1) less than completely decisive for some contemporary interpreters is that the 'phenomena' in view here are described in terms of considerable imaginative 'violence' - the blind abandonment of what is natural and at some level known to be so, and the deliberate turning in rapacity to others. To see this as an account of 'the phenomenon of homosexual behaviour' is to beg the question somewhat...". In other words, what is described there bears little resemblance to the generality of active gay people today. It may be clear what Paul is referring to in that context, but where is the equivalent of it now?

I find a fourth weakness in the traditional approach. There are other Biblical texts which raise important question that I have never found addressed. One of them is Genesis 2:18. What does God's statement, "It is not good for the man to be alone", mean for the genuinely gay person? What does the teaching of Jesus and Paul, that only some have the capacity for celibacy, mean for the gay person? I will come back to that later.

The Relevant Verses

So we turn now to the specific texts which refer to homosexual acts.

Genesis 18:26 and 19:29. Historically this is the passage which has been quoted most frequently. But it is the weakest when it comes to its relevance for today; the story of the destruction of Sodom and Gomorrah.

It is strange that the terms 'sodomy' and 'sodomite' have became alternative terms for homosexual acts and people, but also have become enshrined in the laws of some countries, because the whole Sodom story is a very particular and peculiar one that has probably no parallel in history.

"Revisionist" writers on homosexuality often come to this passage from a very different angle by saying that God's judgement on the cities was primarily because of lack of hospitality for the angelic visitors. Sherwin Bailey helped to popularise this view. This is not as far-fetched as it might sound. There is no question that in Hebrew culture, as in almost the whole of Africa and parts of Asia today, hospitality was a prime requirement and failure to offer it was regarded as a serious offence. In fact Ezekiel 16:49-50 specifically gives this failure to offer hospitality, as well as the city's pride, as the reasons for Sodom's judgement. In that sense revisionist arguments are correct.

Jude 7 however sees the judgement as being because of sexual sin. In Matthew 10:14-15; 11:20-24 Jesus implies that the sin was the refusal to hear God's messengers. It is interesting to note that the sin of Sodom is stated, by Jesus, to be less serious than that of the Galilean town of Capernaum. The truth is that Sodom is a unique situation. Genesis 19:4-5 tells us that "all the men from every part of the city of Sodom, both young and old, surrounded the house". They called to Lot "Where are the men who came to you tonight? Bring them out to us so we can have sex with them."

This is an amazing place if all the people concerned were homosexual by orientation !! "All the men from every part of the city - young and old". How had the city come into existence at all if all the male citizens were genuinely homosexual? But then verse 6 tells us that Lot offered them his virgin daughters as a substitute. Oh - it appears they were bisexual after all! And evidently the safety of his guests was more important than the gang-rape of his daughters (v 8) ! They also threaten Lot with the same treatment, who was evidently not homosexual, and try forcibly to enter his house (v 9).

The only things we can be certain of in this unusual scene are (a) the male citizens of Sodom were as debauched a group of people as any you could find in history, wanting sex in any way they could get it; (b) they were proposing gang-rape, as well as a series of lesser crimes like breaking and entering, and intent to cause grievous bodily harm.

The passage has very little to say for any situation we are likely to be faced with today. There is a parallel incident recorded in Judges 19:23-25 which also involves threatened rape of a male, but in fact leads to the rape and death of a female. Women were always more expendable it seems. Again, this suggests that the men concerned were not homosexual by nature.

Leviticus 18:22 and 20:13. The first says "Do not lie with a man as one lies with a woman, that is detestable". The second adds that they must be put to death for the offence. This is frequently the verse that anti-gay protesters display on banners, not surprisingly, because it appears to be clear and simple.

I am going to spend some time on these verses because their 'apparent' clarity can be very misleading. It is not my purpose to try and explain away what it says. Its meaning is clear in the context in which it is given. But a little thought makes it plain that it is not quite so simple in its application for today. A cursory reading of the other instructions given in the same chapters makes this evident. In Chapter 19 there are instructions not to "plant your field with two kinds of seed", and not to "wear clothing woven of two kinds of material " (v 19); not to "eat meat with the blood still in it" (v 26), not to "cut the hair at the sides of your head or clip off the edges of your beard" (v27) and not to "have tattoos" (v 28.)

I'm in deep trouble. Apart from the fact that I don't plant any crops, I am guilty of all the other forbidden practices, including my two tattoos. Clearly there are factors here that are not immediately obvious to the 21st century reader. Some of the commands don't make any sense today. Almost all of us have some pieces of clothing made up of more than one fibre. The garment is sometimes improved by doing this. Whatever, the mixing is not a moral issue. For us the way we cut our hair, or whether we wear a beard, is not a moral issue.

So the teaching in Leviticus is clearly for circumstances at that time. It has no application to today. It is a principle of Biblical hermeneutics that texts which speak to issues in the past, which have no counterpart today, have to be used with great care. The text cannot be used to command something today, in circumstances where there is no contemporary equivalent.

Preachers often do take texts, of course, and weave a sermon from them that is unrelated to what the verse was originally teaching. If this is legitimate at all (and that is questionable) it is only legitimate if what is being taught is found unambiguously in other parts of Scripture. I suggest, therefore, that the Leviticus verses cannot be used as 'primary' instruction on homosexuality. It only has a primary meaning if it can be proved that the verses are intended to be a command from God for all time, and all situations.

There is a long list of forbidden relationships in Chapter 18, and of sexual sins in Chapter 20, which do have parallels today. But then we notice that the penalty for these sins was frequently death. Again, we find ourselves in somewhat foreign territory. Fundamentalist Muslims do in fact seek to apply these scriptures today, and get into great difficulty because of it.

Christians would find it totally contrary to the spirit of New Testament teaching to apply capital punishment to adulterers and homosexuals. It would be illegal in the countries of Europe, where capital punishment has been abolished. That in itself gives us some clues. Capital punishment is commanded for a good many things in the Old Testament, and sanctioned by Romans 13:4 in the New Testament. But most Christians, including those who regard the whole Bible as inspired by God, would support the abolition of the death penalty.

For one thing the conditions are very different. In the complexities of modern nations it has been too easy for mistakes to be made, and the innocent put to death. We are also aware that in a world where poverty abounds, and the poor are sometimes driven to crime, more often than not it is the poor who are found sitting on Death Row. Context, culture, time and place - do make a difference to our application.

The list of sexual offences in Leviticus sometimes makes curious reading, because listed with adultery and incest we find child sacrifice, bestiality and intercourse with a menstruating woman. If the lists in their totality represent what was happening in society then, we get a picture not much less debauched than Sodom. It's hard to identify this with Israel, never mind the societies in which we now live.

Robert Arthur in his book "Homosexuality and the Conservative

Christian" suggests we have in these lists activities frequently related to the worship of Molech.(cf Leviticus 18:21) "We must remember that the Levitical law was given to the people of Israel as they were travelling through hostile territory where the inhabitants were all idolaters. The major god of these desert people was Molech, a fire god. The major thrust of God's instructions to Israel is summed up well in Leviticus 18:3, the introduction to this legislation, "You must not do as they do in Egypt, where you used to live, and you must not do as they do in the land of Canaan, where I am bringing you. Do not follow their practices". Bestiality, child sacrifice, idolatry, beard trimming, tattooing, menstrual intercourse, were amongst their practices. Extreme measures were taken, even to the point of capital punishment, because of the extreme circumstances and danger to which Israel was exposed.

A great many of the instructions of the first five book of the Bible were for a particular people, in a particular place at a particular time. Some were to protect from moral sins, some to protect from religious (i.e. ceremonial) sins and some were to protect from physical dangers. Many instructions given about eating and hygiene were to protect them from sickness and disease in their special circumstances as Bedouins. In Deuteronomy 23:17 we find a strong command not to become involved in shrine prostitution, either female or male. Earnings from such practices were not acceptable for offerings in the house of the Lord. Shrine prostitution was undoubtedly something that had entered the life of Israel through too close involvement with heathen nations around them. Leviticus 18:22 and 20:13 have to be seen in this wider context of association with forbidden heathen practices and religion. Clearly what is forbidden is something very serious, especially as it incurred the death penalty. One possibility is that it is intercourse with temple-prostitute-priests that is being condemned in the Leviticus texts.

It will help us to understand the extent to which these Old Testament passages have application today, if we explain more fully the law codes given in the early books of the Bible. It's not an exaggeration to say that the failure to distinguish sufficiently between the different codes has caused havoc in the history of the Christian Church. I could expand on this at length, but I won't because it is controversial and is not directly related to our subject.

The question is "How much should we look for a pattern in the Old Testament for New Covenant Church life?" A parallel question is "How much should we look to the Old Testament for instruction on the government of nations? Briefly, there are three kinds of law found in the first five books of the Bible:

> (a) Laws which were permanent and universal, as seen in particular in the Ten Commandments.

> (b) Laws for governing the religious life of Israel. These were not permanent in the particular form in which they were given, though they expressed some permanent and universal truths. For example, the Temple was central to the religious life of Israel; it was made according to a pattern commanded by God. But Jesus announced its destruction and replacement by a temple of an entirely different nature, his church made up of living stones, people. The commands concerning the construction of the Jerusalem Temple have no practical relevance today.

> (c) Laws for the regulation of the life of Israel as a nation. They laid down a judicial system for dealing with various offences and gave regulations for the domestic life of the nation, such as every society needs for its own good order and welfare. These laws may sometimes reflect the permanent moral laws of God, as expressed in the Ten Commandments. Almost all nations forbid stealing and murder and impose heavy penalties. But they do not usually legislate on adultery. Fundamentalist Muslim States do, but that is precisely because they fail to distinguish between the different kinds of Law in the Old Testament. Christians see adultery as a sin but not a crime. It is a matter for the

Church's discipline not the State's. The distinction exists because under the Old Covenant, Israel the Church and Israel the State were one, two faces of the same body. Under the New Covenant Jesus separated them once and for all when he gave the instruction, "Give to Caesar what is Caesar's, and to God what is God's" (Matthew 22:21). Because Church and State were one in the Old Testament the various codes governing the moral, ecclesiastical and political, often overlap and are not easily distinguishable. But just as the ecclesiastical laws were changeable and not permanent, and were eventually superseded with the coming of Jesus, so likewise with the laws regulating the life of the nation. We in our society, deal with poverty and social problems in a different way. Our economic systems are very different. The Old Testament food laws no longer apply. The Christian can enjoy his roast pork, with apple sauce. Nations are free to change their laws as is appropriate. One nation differs from another in its laws, some are appropriate for one situation, not for another, some have the death penalty, some don't. These laws are neither permanent nor universal.

This leaves us, of course, with the problem of deciding to which of these categories the instruction of Leviticus 18:22 belongs. That, to an extent, depends on how much the existence of such laws was determined by circumstances peculiar to that time. There is no final proof, but I am suggesting it is 'highly likely'.

Robin Scroggs in his book *"The New Testament and Homosexuality"* suggests another factor that makes the Leviticus verses commands for a particular time and a particular place. Wasting semen was regarded as a sin in the Old Testament (Genesis 38:9-10). Semen was intended for procreation. To waste semen was a sin, not only because it was the means to life, but because large families were a blessing from God. They were a reward for righteousness, whereas barrenness was viewed as a consequence of sinfulness. That's why we see men like Abraham going to extremes to produce a son and heir, when he had intercourse with his barren wife's maid. Genesis 38 describes Onan trying to avoid producing more children (on behalf of his dead brother), for which he would have been responsible, by spilling his semen. Verse 10 says "What he did was wicked in the Lord's sight; so he put him to death". A man's semen was seen as the 'seed of life'. The woman was only the 'incubator', a very different understanding from today.

Wasting of semen is no longer seen as a sin, anymore than most Christians regard birth control as a sin. The earth no longer 'needs to be filled'; much of it is overpopulated. Scroggs suggests that the strength of opposition to homosexuality in Leviticus 18 and 20 has its roots, at least partly, in the desire to protect the sacredness of life.

Where does this leave us? Many 'revisionists' will probably say, "Problem solved". I think that is going too far. We cannot be sure that the command of God in the Leviticus verses does not have an element of the permanent and universal in it. We cannot give all the benefit of the doubt to those who argue for the legitimacy of same sex acts in certain circumstances. But there is serious doubt as to the intention of these verses and whether they have any application today. *It should be enough to make those who hold traditional views hesitate.* I think it means that as Genesis 18 has nothing to contribute to the current debate, and the circumstances of Leviticus are so special, the Old Testament gives us no primary help in the current debate.

I am going to spend less time on the New Testament passages, not because they are less important but because they are more straightforward. There are really only two passages we need to look at, because other references are very brief and don't add anything new. I'm going to leave Romans 1 until the last, because it is the most difficult to answer.

1 Corinthians 6:9-11 "Do you not know that the wicked will not inherit the kingdom of God? Do not be deceived; neither the sexually immoral nor idolaters nor adulterers nor male prostitutes nor homosexual offenders nor thieves nor the greedy nor drunk nor slanderers nor swindlers will inherit the kingdom of God. And that is what some of you were. But you were washed, you were sanctified, you were justified in the name of the Lord Jesus Christ and by the Spirit of God".

There are a number of issues here, but the big one is the context. It is not enough to say that Paul makes a statement condemning 'homosexual offenders', and then read present-day understanding of what that means back into the text of Scripture. It is not enough to ask "What does Paul say?" We need to ask also, "What did he mean when he said it? What was in his mind?"

One thing we can be certain of is that he did not have in mind people whose sexual orientation was homosexual, because he says (v 11) "and that is what some of you were"; suggesting they were that no longer. He is speaking entirely of sexual acts, whatever they were. Those acts were also wicked enough to rob them of an inheritance in the Kingdom of God. It faces me with an immediate experiential question. How is it that I know so many people who are homosexual, who engage in same-sex acts, but they are Christians who have clear signs of being indwelt by the Holy Spirit? If they have no part in the Kingdom of God the Holy Spirit should have left them long ago. It's another case of a traditional understanding of Scripture simply not fitting the facts.

What did Paul have in mind then? One only has to think of the church, and city, to which he was writing to begin to get the picture. Corinth was the sexual cesspit of the Hellenic world of that time. It was a cosmopolitan port at the hub of major trade routes. We all know what tends to happen in cities with large mobile populations, especially sea-ports where sailors quickly come and go. Corinth had become a byword for licentiousness.

The moral looseness had evidently invaded the Corinthian church, as we see from chapter five as well as six. Fertility worship was found all around the eastern Mediterranean. It corrupted male and female, young and old. There seems to have been no limit to the depravity which idolatry opened up to worshippers of these gods. In the 1 Corinthians 6 list of offences there are two words used in the Greek to refer to homosexual acts. In some translations they have been combined to make it one offence. In the NIV they are correctly kept separate and translated 'male prostitutes nor homosexual offenders'.

The first need not refer to homosexuals at all, but probably does because of the context. The literal meaning of the Greek word malakoi is 'soft', i.e. effeminate. In context it almost certainly refers to the passive partner in male prostitution, whether cult prostitution or a rent boy. The second term arsenokoitai is extremely rare, but used twice in the New Testament, 1 Corinthians 6 and 1Timothy 4:10. It is reasonable to interpret it, in this context, as referring to sexual acts between men. But before we make too quick an application to the practices of today, we need to understand more of what Paul would have had in mind.

Along with cult prostitution the other common expression of homosexuality, in the Greek world of Paul's day, was pederasty. It was common practice amongst the wealthy upper class, for a rich man to develop a friendship with a good-looking youth, who he would educate but also use for sex. It's not unlike the situation in 18th century England when the Lord of the manor used his stable-boy to 'pleasure himself'. In the Greek context the older man was normally married, under 45 years of age, and the youth a young teenager. A less cultured variation of this was for a very wealthy man to have a 'stable' of handsome slaves who were used for sexual pleasure.

It is clear that the various expressions of sex perversion were so common in Corinth that they were threatening the purity of the church. Some of the members had come from this background (6:11) and were apparently in danger of reverting to it. Perhaps some of them were poor and needed the money. I met a gay man recently, who is undoubtedly a genuine Christian, who when he lost his job and couldn't get another, returned to the prostitution he had practised before conversion. He admitted he had been wrong but went on to say "But how else was I going to pay the rent for my flat?"

We recognise that many females turn to prostitution to feed themselves and their children. Their numbers are large in some of the cities of Africa. There were other sexual sins in the Corinthian Church. Paul had already referred to a case of incest in Chapter 5, and urged the church to 'get rid of the old yeast' (v 7) which was threatening to spread through the whole lump (the body of believers). Along with such serious sexual offences, of which the body needed to be purged, he lists an odd mixture of other sins - not surprisingly - idolatry, but then 'swindlers, slanderers, drunkards and the greedy' (!) It becomes harder and harder to picture this situation and find a modern equivalent.

What form of 'greed' was so bad as to deserve exclusion from the kingdom of God? Or did Paul not accept the kind of gradation of sins which we practice? With obesity at an all time high, there would be many candidates in our churches for exclusion from the kingdom. In the first part of chapter 6 he refers to internal disputes in the fellowship, and tells them that the church was competent to exercise discipline and they did not need to use civil courts. Clearly members had been doing that to settle quarrels among them, so adding to their sins. It gets even harder to picture this church.

Then later in Chapter 6 he reinforces his castigations with a threat that those who persist in wrongdoing will not inherit the kingdom. He strengthens his case with this long list of offences, including prostitutes, homosexual offenders, other sexually immoral people (not defined), idolaters, swindlers, drunkards and thieves! I've once in forty years had to deal with a swindler and thief in the fellowship, but only once. The whole context, in which the reference to homosexual acts appears, is very different from your average church today. Perhaps it's a condemnation of us, that we are simply not touching the lives of the kind of people who the Corinthian church was bringing to Christ, including the more promiscuous wing of the gay community. Add to the complications of this picture, that the homosexual acts referred to were usually performed by men who were not homosexual by nature, but married men with wives. The recipients of the acts were not only paid for it, but sometimes subjected to it involuntarily. So the 'acts' which the Apostle is condemning are being performed in a particularly immoral and idolatrous context.

There appears to be no concept at all of two believing people, homosexual by nature, of a similar age, who had a loving physical relationship. We simply do not know what Paul would have said faced with that kind of situation. He would not have had a problem with close male friendships, even that expressed themselves physically. The Greek world put a great deal of emphasis on close platonic friendship and Paul himself appears to have done so. Amongst African people today it is very acceptable for men to walk down the street holding hands. Standing very close and touching is a normal part of life. It is a sad trend in western society that men are becoming more apprehensive of physical contact with other men - apart from in sport.

Romans 1:26-29. There is no ambiguity in language as to what Paul is referring to. Paul even includes lesbians this time. Men and women were 'exchanging natural relations for unnatural ones'. The men had "abandoned natural relations with women and were inflamed with lust for one another. Men committed indecent acts with other men, and received in themselves the due penalty for their perversion". On the surface it is very clear.

But I come back to the same argument that I have been using. Paul's writings have to be understood in the context from which he wrote. His teaching cannot be applied with confidence to today unless we know that he had a comparable situation in mind. Some writers point out that the Roman letter was written from Corinth and the religious-sexual practices of that city were probably still dominating his thinking. The worship of Aphrodite was the dominant religion, and she was a hermaphrodite with both male and female sexual organs. In the worship of this deity, heterosexual men and women acted out as members of the opposite sex, to experience the sexual side of their deity that differed from their own. They were 'unnatural' acts.

So what Paul was railing against in Romans 1 was sexual orgies of a particularly horrible kind. That is the background of his writing, but in Romans 1 he is extending it to the rawness of the pagan world that stretched beyond the borders of the Roman-Hellenic world. There was some sophistication in Corinth. There is none in this picture of raw heathenism. Romans 1 reflects an even darker and wider scene, that left no place for the true and living God.

Paul makes clear the extreme seriousness in his opening statement of the section that "The wrath of God is being revealed from heaven against all the godlessness and wickedness of men who suppress the truth by their wickedness, since what may be known about God is plain to them, because God has made it plain to them. For since the creation of the world God's invisible qualities - his eternal power and divine nature - have been clearly seen, being understood from what has been made, so that men are without excuse. For although they knew God, they neither glorified him as God nor gave thanks to him, but their thinking became futile and their foolish minds were darkened. Although they claimed to be wise they became fools and exchanged the glory of the immortal God for images made to look like mortal man and birds and animals and reptiles. Therefore God gave them over in the sinful desires of their hearts to....." and then follows the list of sins and practices that God 'gave them over' to, including unnatural relations; (Romans 1:18ff).

There are a number of important things to notice here:

    (a) The prime sin is their 'godlessness' not the evil things they do. In v 18 'godlessness' comes before 'wickedness'. The failure to acknowledge and worship God is always the prime sin. The first three of the Ten Commandments are entirely concerned with that. When Jesus is asked which is the greatest commandment (Matthew 22:36) he replies "Love the Lord your God with all your heart and with all your soul and with all your mind". There is nothing that even approaches that for importance in the Bible, or in the Christian life. As you read the Bible it is amazing the sins that God seems able to tolerate or ignore with his servants. We only have to be reminded of David's terrible sins, of Samson and Rahab.

    (b) The second biggest sin in the Old Testament is idolatry. It's bad enough not to acknowledge God for who he is, but to worship idols, objects made by their own hands, is a heinous crime beyond description. The Old Testament is the story of the unfailing love of Yahweh for his people Israel. But the one thing he cannot tolerate, and always punishes, is idolatry. He is a 'jealous' God, jealous for the love of his people. He will not allow his glory to be given to anyone else or anything else.

    (c) Rejection of God leads to blindness, so that we lose the knowledge we had through creation. (Romans 1:19 and 21b). If we don't respond to God's revelation of himself, we lose it.

    (d) God takes away his restraining hand, 'gives us over' to all the things we have always been capable of but God has restrained us from. At the end of the Book of Revelation (Revelation 22:10ff) Jesus says to John "Let him who does wrong continue to do wrong; let him who is vile continue to be vile; let him who does right continue to do right; and let him who is holy continue to be holy". A time is coming at the end of the age when God's people will be released finally from the crippling effects of sin, and be able to do fully all they've longed to do; while the wicked will be condemned to an eternity in which they do perpetually what they have chosen to do in this life, but without any of the restraint of God's hand.

The 'unnatural acts' in Romans 1, is part of that scene, in which people turn to many wrong things because God has given up on them. People who reject what knowledge they have, and turn to worshipping created things, experience his righteous anger in the here and now. But the worst part of the punishment is that they stop hearing his voice and stop experiencing his restraint. These are the people being described in Romans 1.

The question is "Do God-fearing gay people fit that description?" Can we really say that this chapter is describing the kind of people I am pleading for? If sexual misdemeanours determined our status with God I wonder how many of us would ever get to heaven? While I was living in England for a few years I got a phone call from a pastor friend in South Africa. He blasted me over the phone for my attitude to gay people and particularly quoted Romans 1:32. Even if I did not engage in homosexual acts, he said, I was nonetheless guilty because I 'approved those who practise them'. I have certainly never approved the Godlessness and life-style described in Romans 1.

Many gay writers say that Romans 1 cannot be referring to people who are gay by orientation, because it says the people 'abandoned natural relations with women'. The same is said of erotic relations between women. Gay writers point out that the passage must be referring to heterosexual people who perform homosexual acts because it is only they who do something 'unnatural'. What would be unnatural for gay people would be to try and do what others want them to do, start acting out a heterosexual role.

I accept the argument of evangelical writers who oppose that interpretation, arguing that Paul is referring to 'acts which are not according to nature'; i.e. not according to the way we were created. I am sure that is the way Paul meant us to read it. At the same time it is true, in the light of present day understanding of homosexuality, that for the person who is by orientation homosexual there is nothing unnatural about being physically attracted to the same sex. I have described earlier my own natural aversion to too much physical contact with women. It is difficult for me to imagine having sex with a woman. I have never had it with a man but I have little difficulty in believing I could enjoy sexual relations with the right man, a man I was physically attracted to.

I have noticed that when heterosexual audiences watch movies with gay content, the thing they seem to hate most is two men kissing on the lips. I've twice heard loud revulsion expressed in cinemas. Occasionally I indulge in a chaste kiss on the lips with a gay man. Many gay men do it as the normal form of greeting. But I can think of few physical things I would find more thrilling than to kiss a man as lovers do. That feeling is totally natural to me, beautiful to me, and I feel no sense of guilt or shame saying it.

I did not choose to be like this. For good or bad it's the way I am 'wired up'. I accept that somewhere in my genetic past the wires got mixed up, but that is the reality for me, that is what is 'natural'. I, and others like me, do not fit the Romans 1 description of having 'abandoned natural relations with women'. How can I abandon what I've never had, never been able to do? This is our problem in applying Romans 1 today, as with the other passages.

The passages are all in the context of 'choice' not orientation.

Two Other Passages

Before closing this chapter I want to turn to two other passages that are not normally discussed, passages I've already mentioned.

It is Not Good to Be Alone

In the creation story, in Genesis 2:18, God is described as looking at Adam and saying, "It is not good for the man to be alone. I will make him a helper suitable for him". It is clear that God is not just talking about man's need for a partner to procreate, or someone on the scene to 'hang out' with. The process by which the woman was created (v 21-25) suggests something more. It is a picture of intimacy, the most intense and enjoyable part of a true marriage relationship.

The semi-serious American gay magazine, *The Advocate*, once did a detailed survey of readers' views on their sexuality. A third of the readership filled in the lengthy questionnaire, a very high response level. The question that intrigued me most was the one that asked, "If you had to choose between sex without love or love without sex, which would you choose?" More than eighty per cent of the respondents said "Love without sex".

There is something in human beings that cries out for love, not just in a general sense, but in deep intimate relationship with another human being. Through my job I have been shown a lot of love by a lot of people. I have a circle of closer friends whose practical love for me, sometimes over many years, fills me with amazement and gratitude. Some of them know just about the worst about me and still seem to love me unconditionally. I have also had a very meaningful and fulfilling life. I look back with real satisfaction at what God has done. But there is one area in which I am unfulfilled. I have never known the kind of intimacy I am writing about. At the centre of my being there is a void, a pain, that cries out for it. I can only handle it because Christ lives in me by His Spirit, and he shares that pain.

Of course I am not the only person in that position. Nor are gay people, who remain celibate, the only ones in that position. Any pastor knows of fine Christian women who have gone to the ends of the earth as missionaries, and part of the price has been singleness. There are Christian women, and some men, in every congregation, for whom there is no partner because they refuse to marry a non-Christian. But I don't think I've ever met a single person who didn't hope that Mr Right or Miss Right might still come along. I've been in retirement homes, where the competition amongst the female majority for the attention of the few males, was intense. Hope springs eternal!

But what about the teenager who loves the Lord, wants to be faithful, but knows he/she is gay? He seeks counsel from his pastor. He tells him he is gay, and also tells him that he has a gay friend to whom he is attracted. The pastor listens to his story and is eventually convinced that the young man is homosexual by orientation. He is a good pastor, he assures him that God still loves him and the church accepts him, with one proviso. He must be celibate; he must curb his sexual urges, whatever that involves. He must not take the risk of physical contact with his friend. It would be wiser to break the friendship altogether. It doesn't matter if he lives to the age of a hundred he can never know the kind of intimacy I have been describing. He must not only be celibate, he must be as if he were a eunuch. The pastor tries to cushion the blow by encouraging him to develop other friendships in the church.

Try to imagine how the young man, or woman, feels. He's a typical teenager, his hormones are hyper-active. But it's not just a matter of 'waiting' in his case, like most heterosexual teenagers. *It is never*.

Let's assume he does have heterosexual teenage friends, who accept him as he is. One by one those friends will pair off, and eventually get married. He is no longer even John's best friend. The married John has someone else now who is closer. His loneliness is intensified and the inner cry for intimacy becomes intolerable. For all his commitment to Christ he is still spiritually immature, not able to carry the burdens that only a life-time of walking with Christ makes possible. He feels he can't even talk about it with most of his friends, because they won't understand. What does "It is not good for man to be alone" mean for him? How does God's loving provision manifest itself in his life? Didn't God have people like him in mind when he made that statement and promise to Adam?

What is likely to happen in this situation, because it is not an infrequent one? In a few cases - suicide. The suicide rate amongst gay teenagers is three times higher than amongst straight teenagers. In far more cases he simply leaves the church, decides God has no good purpose for him, and gets on with his life. The possibility of spending seventy, eighty more years on earth without intimacy is too much of a price to pay. He prefers to take his chances on Judgement Day, trusting that God will be more gracious than the church says he is, to people like him. In some cases he will go to a non-evangelical church where they seem to have more compassion; or a gay church if there's one in the area. But in the majority of cases he just drifts away, not because he's rejected God but because he feels God's church has rejected him, by setting the hurdles too high. I know so many young people like this. Their faces are flashing through my mind; and I feel tremendous sorrow and some anger.

Celibacy

The other passages I want to refer to deal with celibacy. We've noticed already Matthew 19 where Jesus is questioned about divorce. He states firmly that divorce was not part of God's original purpose for people and was only permitted when there had been marital unfaithfulness (v 8-9).

The disciples were astonished by the hardness of this teaching and say, "If this is the situation between a husband and wife, it is better not to marry" (v 10). Jesus says they are going too far. Just as marriage can be difficult, so can singleness. It is not a possibility for everyone; it is a gift. (v 11). "Jesus replied, not everyone can accept this word, but only those to whom it has been given". Then he describes those for whom celibacy is right or a possibility, (v 12). "For some are eunuchs because they were born that way; others were made that way by men; and others have renounced marriage because of the kingdom of heaven. The one who can accept this should accept it".

It's intriguing to speculate what he meant by some "were born that way"? I doubt if it implies that Jesus understood that some people are born homosexual, unable to marry. But that's not impossible. When I was young people who lived in my blue-collar community used to talk about some folk not being 'the marrying kind'. They probably meant homosexual, but their thoughts were not so clearly defined as that. I think Jesus is simply saying that some people have no choice, whatever the reason. Maybe they are people born with a deformity that makes marriage impossible. Others were made that way, often against their choice - castrated. But some have been 'given the gift; and use it for the sake of the kingdom.

But there is clearly the inference that some can't and shouldn't try. Paul says something similar in 1 Corinthians 7. He starts by saying that it is good for a man not to marry (v 1). He is making clear that singleness is an acceptable condition. But he is also making clear (v 26-31) that it was to be recommended at that time because of special difficulties that existed; in other words for a particular people, in a particular place, at a particular time. He then turns to those who marry and says that when they do they should not deny their partners their marital rights (v 3-6); i.e. their sexual rights. They should not marry and then try and live as if they were single and celibate. Each state is legitimate, but each also has its responsibilities. Each person has to decide which 'gift' God has given him. If someone chooses not to marry but then finds he does not have the gift, cannot handle celibacy, he should marry (v 9). It is better to marry than to be constantly troubled with lust and temptation.

So, both Jesus and Paul make very clear that as some cannot handle marriage, not everyone can handle celibacy. But the big question for us becomes; how does this work out in the case of gay people, those who are homosexual by orientation? There is a similar cross-section amongst homosexual people, when it comes to testosterone levels, as with heterosexuals. But heterosexuals have a choice. According to the traditional evangelical approach to homosexuality, homosexuals have no choice. Some will have the 'celibacy gift', as some heterosexuals do.

I confess I sometimes wonder about this idea of it being a 'gift'. It makes it sound so easy. But it's not for me. I've coped but I don't know whether I have the 'gift'. It certainly doesn't feel like it! These Scripture passages make clear that some will not have the gift. Some may use that as a convenient excuse. But Scripture is emphatic that for some it will be the truth; they 'burn', as Paul puts it. I think I've made my point. I would be interested to hear an answer to this particular point. I assume the answer will include a lot of cold showers, hard exercise and an incredible level of spiritual maturity and sanctification, of the kind that doesn't come overnight. Those, of course, who believe all gay people can be healed or cured will say otherwise. But less and less people see that as a realistic possibility for the majority of gay folk.

What Does Jesus Say?

I've tried to deal with the Old Testament and New Testament texts. But there is another part of Scripture, and another teacher, we have barely mentioned - the four gospels and Jesus. What do the gospels say about homosexuality? What does Jesus say?

Is it of no significance that virtually nothing is said? Can we at least accept that Jesus evidently doesn't put it as high on his agenda as evangelicals tend to do?

Let me finish this bit, with quoting from Tony Campolo again. "Jesus undoubtedly knew about homosexuality, and we can assume that he held to the teachings of the Torah on the subject. But nowhere did He condemn gays and lesbians. In fact, Jesus never mentioned homosexuality. It just wasn't on his Top Ten list of sins. Number one on the list, however, are judgemental religious people who look for sin in the lives of others without dealing with the sin in their own lives (Matthew 23). It is uncomfortable to note that although Jesus was silent about homosexuality, He did specifically condemn the remarriage of divorced people unless adultery was the cause of the divorce. Nevertheless, most contemporary Christians accept the remarriage of divorced persons regardless of the bases of their divorces. Gays often ask why evangelicals seem willing to accept couples who are divorced and remarried, a sexual relationship that Jesus specifically condemned as adultery, then come down so hard on a sexual relationship that Jesus never mentioned. It's not that gays condemn remarried divorced persons, but only that gays are asking that they not be condemned and that the church show as much grace to them". Tony Campolo, like myself, does not claim to know all the answers, but he does have a very good overall perspective from which we can all learn.

Chapter Seven - Change begins in the home

When my friend pressurised me to write this book he included, in his suggested outline, chapters on parents and children. I protested that as a single gay man I didn't have enough worth saying on parenting. His answer was one I've used myself. A life-time of pastoring people of all shapes and sizes often leaves someone like me with a more objective insight, into the problems of marriage and parenting, than those directly involved.

I've often been asked, when counselling couples with marriage problems, how I know so much about marriage. If I do, it's not primarily because of reading books or listening to lectures. It's mainly because, having listened to a few people's stories, you find yourself pretty well equipped for understanding the rest. It never ceases to amaze me how humanity has this ability to go on repeating the same mistakes over and over again.

This also applies to parenting. I've not only pastored and worked with hundreds of families; I've been privileged to have large numbers of young people under my pastoral care. As a result I've been able to come to a few conclusions. Most young people who come for counselling are battling with the same issues as their contemporaries. As a wise man of old once said (Ecclesiastes 1:9), "What has been will be again, what has been done will be done again, there is nothing new under the sun" ! So you've got to be pretty stupid if you've spent hours counselling people, or just spent years growing old, if you haven't learned a few lessons. So let me share a few things I've observed. And I claim no infallibility.

Parenting is Tough and Difficult

Bringing up kids is difficult, very difficult. Some might say - near impossible. Good parenting means years of sacrifice and self-denial. In these days when people tend to get married later, and then delay having children, retirement is almost upon them by the time the children leave the nest. I often wonder where these older parents find the energy.

So it's not difficult to understand why parents are disappointed when things don't turn out as they had hoped and planned. So much has been invested in time and energy, never mind the money. Every parent has a mental image of their kids' future, and they don't include the gay option. That's not one of the 'disappointments' they'd prepared for. That happens to other people.

Only last week I was talking with a dad who has two adopted children. For ten years he's had a serious problem making a living, losing his capital in failed businesses, uprooting and moving overseas hoping for a better start, doing jobs that he hated in order to put bread on the table, struggling with loss of self-respect because he feels he's failed himself and his family. He described himself as 'having been to hell and back'. He knew that there would be additional problems bringing up adopted children. But he wasn't prepared for finding out that his twelve year old son is showing the signs of being gay. The kids at school have already picked it up. His wife is battling even more with the idea. They are evangelical Christians, so have a background of 'gay' being a negative word. The boy showed early signs of a commitment to Christ. But now he wants nothing to do with church; possibly because he's already picked up that gay and God are not supposed to go together.

The toughest stage in bringing up kids by far is teenage. Some mum's might argue that the early years are the most demanding, especially if there is more than one child and their ages are close. I had an associate pastor whose wife had triplets. Three had not been expected. The ultra-sound had not brought it up. So they were unprepared for the extent to which their lives would be disrupted. Watching the tiredness, stress and sometimes anger at her circumstances, left me speechless at what mothers can go through. But I still think there is a difference between handling that kind of stress, which has a limited time span, to handling the problems of teenagers.

One of my mother's many woeful observations on life was "They make your arms ache when they are little, but they make your heart ache when they grow up"! She used it to make my sister and me feel guilty, to bring us into line. Of course it irritated us no end. But it has a grain of truth. It's easier to handle the physical pressure than the inner disappointments. I've no doubt of it - teenage years are the really difficult ones for most. The petty, pouting arguments of earlier years are nothing compared to the rebellions when hormones start raging and the process of preparing to leave the nest begins. Because that is what is happening. It is often hard for parents to recognise and accept it. But children are going to leave the nest and they need to do it, for everybody's good. And it shouldn't be delayed too long; that has its problem as well. All the painful stages of teenage are a preparation for it.

So those few years often seem like a never-ending roller-coaster ride. The changes, the mood swings, the fads and crazes make it look as if sweet Susie or cute Tommy is fast developing into an uncontrollable monster or lunatic. How could upright, hard-working parents, as you are, have produced such rebels against society? And often this frustration and disappointment is accompanied by guilt. John White deals with it so well in his excellent book "Parents in Pain". Every parent who is crying out "What did I do wrong?" should read it.

Keen Christian Teenagers

But even if you have teenage children who don't seem to be going through any of this, watch out! I'm more nervous about kids who are too serious about life and God too early.

It's part of emerging into adulthood that you go through all the typical uncertainties and adjustments. The teenager who doesn't appear to be having these difficulties sometimes goes through a much more serious crisis later. It's one of the reasons why it's unwise to push young people into spiritual commitments for which they are not yet ready. They are much more likely to become disappointed with God, and spiritually disabled.

A preacher friend of mine recently told me how disappointed he was that his oldest son had turned his back on God after doing so well spiritually in his earlier years. He traced it back to the sudden and tragic death of his son's close teenage friend. Teenagers don't handle death well. They are supposed to 'live for ever'. Friends are also extremely important for teenagers. For years his son had listened attentively to his dad preaching about the joys and satisfaction of following God; how God takes care of his children. He loved and respected his dad as a man and as a preacher. If his dad said something important it must be true. Now, he felt let down by his dad as well as God. Preacher's kids have a particularly hard time; they know too much too early.

So Christian leaders can really beat themselves to death over their failures with their kids. Doesn't Paul tell Timothy (1 Timothy 3:4) that they must 'manage their own family well'? And there are always people in the church who keep that weapon up their sleeve, to use it on the pastor when they are especially mad with him. But as John White points out, there are no perfect parents, as there are no perfect children. It is not God's will for Christian parents to beat themselves up over their mistakes. Doing that sometimes leads them to make more. To overcompensate, for instance, and start spoiling the kids too much.

Kids are good at using parental guilt to get their own way. The parents may also be so preoccupied with their own failures that they can't see what the kids are going through inwardly. Two weeks ago I stayed with long-time friends who I first knew as missionaries in Africa. I met two of their married children who I had last seen when they were very young, more than thirty years ago. I asked them how they had coped being missionary kids, especially in their teens. They both described the anger and resentment they had gone through against their parents, and against God, because they had been dragged from their homeland to a strange country, because it was "God's will". At sixteen the daughter had been so angry that she left home. As they approach middle life they are now well settled in their faith and in God's Church. But there was still some anger coming out of the daughter as she described how she had felt.

I could see some of the embarrassment and pain her parents felt as she spoke. I know them as very good people, the 'salt of the earth' kind of Christians. I was sorry that I had raised questions that caused them obvious hurt, hurt which was undeserved. They reacted well, as with honesty and humility they accepted they had made mistakes. But they also patiently explained that they had genuinely done what they believed to be right at that time, not only toward God but for the children as well. I encouraged them to believe that. It's easy to see by hindsight that we didn't get it right. We each have to act with our best insights in the circumstances of the time. God doesn't expect more.

In their case the imperfect efforts to be the best parents they could be had a good end result. But John White argues that there is no certain connection between the quality of the parenting and the end result. God gives every man and woman the freedom to make choices and mistakes. Children have the same choices and some of the bad ones they make are not obviously attributable to the quality of the parenting. I've observed that some very average Christian parents have brought up kids who all become fine Christians. But I've also got Christian friends for whom my heart aches. They are as dedicated, wise, loving as any parents could be but their kids have turned out to be godless; for the moment anyway.

Parents, of all people, need faith to go on praying and believing. When a fourteen year old says he doesn't want to go to church anymore he is not necessarily turning his back on God. He's saying he wants to start making more of his own decisions. And that's an important part of the growing up process.

Don't Panic

The number one mistake I've observed parents making during the roller-coaster teen years is to panic. This often leads to over reaction and bigger mistakes. They begin to major too much on minors and read too much into fashions and fads. A friend whose pastor husband died suddenly, leaving her with three teenage children, asked me if I would be willing to give some 'fathering' to the sixteen year old boy. I agreed because he and I seemed to have a good relationship. It involved little more than getting together from time to time for coffee, or a milk-shake, so that he could share what was happening in his life.

On one occasion he asked "What do you think about tattoos?" Teenagers respect honesty from adults, perhaps more than anything. So I replied that I had no strong feelings on the subject, provided it was done by a reputable and safe tattooist. I added that I had often thought of having one myself. It was the truth, and I acted on it later. The following Sunday, in church, I could see his mother was mad with me. She had urged him to come to me because she was sure I would discourage him. "Then you don't really know me" I said. "It really isn't the big issue you are making it. It's no more than a fashion statement. But such statements can be important to teenagers. The more you fight a teenager on secondary issues the more likely he is to do something much more questionable.

If you want to worry about him, worry about the threat of drugs or something really harmful that he might get into." When he did finally get his tattoo it was one he had designed himself, as a tribute to his dad who he loved and respected very much. The mother was deeply moved.

Recently I watched a dad arriving at a cricket match with two young teenage daughters. They were both clad, or unclad, in the current rage - hipster jeans separated from their tops by six inches of bare belly, and a stud piercing the belly button. With a few girls it can be attractive even if provocative. With many it's not, because of the flab even teenagers carry these days, when overeating is the norm. It looked so awful to me that I found myself wishing the dad would tell them to cover up. It was putting me off my appetite for my sandwiches! But then I realised he was probably being wise. It can be terribly important to a teenage girl not to be different from her peers. The great thing is - the fashion will soon have changed anyway!

Obviously there are limits, for Christian parents in particular. But sometimes Christians are less wise than their non-Christian counterparts, in recognising what is a passing fad and what is fundamental. For all their rebelliousness, teenagers are very insecure people who desperately need to be understood, loved and affirmed, not criticised. Last evening I was watching the American version of 'Idols', the talent competition that looks for the best pop singer in Britain, America, South Africa or one of several other countries. The finalists are chosen from thousands who sing, or try to sing, their way through the early rounds. Those rounds leave you marvelling at the human capacity for self-deception. The performances last night were in the main awful; and the whole thing was well lubricated with the usual amount of American schmaltz. The contestants are nearly always supported by lots of family members and friends who comfort them and pick up the pieces when they are turned down. And there are often a lot of pieces to be picked up.

So one sixteen year old boy was asked why he was on his own. He looked very sad but explained that his parents didn't seem to understand his passion for singing and the amount of money it cost for all the training and travelling. But there was no bitterness or accusation. He seemed a really nice, quiet sort of kid. The judges were surprised at the power and range of his voice and had no hesitation in sending him on to the finals in Hollywood. His surprise and excitement was delightful. He grabbed his cell phone and rang his mother. It ended with tears rolling down his face as he shouted "My mum's proud of me". I think it meant as much to find his mother could be proud of him as it did to get through to the finals. Teenagers cry out to be affirmed, especially by their parents.

"Mum, Dad, I'm Gay"

All I've written so far in this chapter has been to highlight the context of the situation when a teenager says to parents, "Mum, Dad, I'm gay". The reality is, of course, that they are unlikely to volunteer that information, particularly if the parents are evangelical Christians. Depending on their age they have probably known for some time that they are different from other kids and that's very scary. Being part of the pack is very important for the teenager. In some cases they've already been bullied at school, and even called 'sissy' as I was, or "fag", "poof", "homo", a few of a variety of terms that strike like a deep cutting knife. There was never a more untrue saying than "Sticks and stones may break my bones, but words can never hurt me". Words do hurt.

Our teenager has already become aware of his attraction to particular young people, movie stars or sports stars. But it's often difficult to know the difference between a 'crush' and something more than that. The term 'crush' is normally associated with schoolgirls, but boys have them too. Maybe they hadn't noticed, to begin with, that the attraction is to the same sex. It's common and normal for teenagers to have a lot of physical contact, so the line between what is sexual and what is just male bonding gets blurred. But as time goes by, and their peers begin to pair off with the opposite sex, a gulf begins to develop between them and others. They become aware that they are different and it starts to get very lonely out there.

At the same time new feelings begin to develop, exciting feelings, for others of the same sex. They become aware of a strong physical attraction to certain types, the sporting jocks or the studious types. But to look even for two seconds too long at that well built guy in the locker room is very risky. It's likely to result in an angry response, maybe even a punch. Things are changing, even if slowly, in non-Christian society. Society as a whole is becoming much more accepting. Through teachers, and the media, homophobia is now frequently condemned. It's seen as being in the same category as racism or sexism.

If the gay teenager happens to be good-looking, good at sport, good in class, generally likeable, there is a fair chance these days he/she will be accepted. But they are the lucky ones. Gay boys are often not good at sport, especially at ball games. It's been a nightmare for me, at church picnics or camps, finding a ball that is asking to be caught or kicked coming in my direction. I can't throw over-arm and the ball has a way of going in the wrong direction when I kick it! This doesn't normally apply to girls who are gay. In the past they got very frustrated at not being allowed to play games thought to be a male preserve. That's all changed. But lesbian girls often get ridiculed for not being feminine enough, too butch. But all this has led to many gay kids having low self-esteem and that doesn't give them the confidence to make friends easily. Life is frequently extra hard for gay teenagers. Teen years are difficult anyway, without all these additional problems. No wonder the suicide rate is so much higher amongst gay teens.

But then there come all the more difficult problems that gay teenagers have to face in a Christian home, and have to face with the church folk who form part of their family social background. Non-Christians eventually get used to having gay kids. Many of them have little or no problem in these changed times. But there is no guarantee that will be the case in a Christian home or church.

Most gay teens from Christian homes already know what the church says, particularly if it is conservative in theology. Some pastors in evangelical churches preach as if there were no gay folk in their congregations. They wouldn't dare show their faces, or soil our carpets. So they don't spare their words in describing what the Bible says about these 'abominations'. When a few years ago, a well-known preacher in Britain revealed he was gay, another preacher I know declared in no uncertain terms, that this man was on his way to hell. I listened to the tape of the sermon.

There are many more moderate preachers who wouldn't be so crude, or uncharitable, but make snide remarks that deeply offend gay people in their congregations. I've referred already to a conversation I had with a young gay man in a church where I was speaking. I believed his pastor to be a man with real compassion for gays, and I urged the young man to 'come out' to his pastor. "Oh no" said the lad, "recently he mimicked, in one of his sermons, a gay man carrying a handbag". No doubt it was done for a cheap laugh, rather than an intended attack.

On the few occasions I've heard my own pastor mention the subject, it has always been with the feeling that he cares about the difficulties gay people face. Even if a pastor has strong views about homosexual practice he should still speak with understanding and compassion. Even if I was straight I don't think I would want to be in a church where the pastor appeared to lack compassion for the needy, for failures, for misfits. The kind of church where it seems to be more important to prove you are 'sound', standing firmly for 'the truth' in a relativistic age. I'm afraid I've sometimes been that kind of preacher in the past.

Poor gay teenager - who has to sit under that kind of ministry; and unfortunately many do. It's time more Christian parents, and Christians in general, told their pastors what they feel about such attitudes. People sometimes keep quiet because they don't want to be seen as 'rebels against the truth'. When I 'came out' in Reading, I was surprised at some of the folk in the church who said they had been waiting for years for an evangelical to speak out against traditional thinking on this subject.

Things are changing but there are still many teenagers, who when they realise they are gay, take it for granted that their church and their parents will be against them. They 'know' what those Scriptures say. Those teens who have already committed themselves to Christ have a genuine respect for the Bible, the pastor and the faith of their parents. They often believe without question that the Bible allows no space for gay people in the Kingdom of God. Only a full repentance from and rejection of, every thought, attitude and practice associated with homosexuality, gives them any hope of salvation. That is the clear message preached in most evangelical churches.

I have talked with Christian gay people, young and older, who because of their church background are completely convinced they are damned to hell - even though they do love God. If someone like me suggests that the Bible message is not so clearly defined, I am likely to be met with scepticism and possibly lose their respect. "Doesn't the Bible say it clearly?" I talked recently with an older Christian woman who used to be a missionary, who hasn't been to church regularly for years. I was once her pastor and had a good idea she was gay, and in a relationship with another woman that was more than just friendship. The opportunity came to discuss it with her. I told her my own story hoping that I could persuade her that she was not rejected by God. But she came from a strong fundamentalist home. Her stepfather, for whom she had little respect, was a pastor and clearly it had been drummed into her for years that there is no place in heaven for gay people.

Our conversation revealed that she hadn't had sexual contact with another woman for many years. But she still felt guilty and thought I was compromising in telling her that God still loved her. It didn't seem to occur to her that God might be more concerned about the fact she no longer worshipped him, or had regular fellowship with other Christian people. That is one of the results of evangelical preachers making homosexuality a sin in a category of its own.

So, the Christian teenager is frequently faced not only with rejection by his peers but condemnation at home and in church. But most of all he is faced with a presentation of the Gospel, that appears to say God hates him, even though he genuinely wants to love God. It doesn't help him much to tell him that God hates the sin, but loves the sinner. He finds it difficult to separate the two. Though he may not yet have physically committed the sin, in his heart and mind he has often done so, and didn't Jesus say that the thought is as bad as the deed? He wants to love and serve God, but he is not just a spiritual being. The teenager is very aware of his physicality. He is full of energy, prefers 'doing' things rather than more passive occupations. He likes being with people of his own age. He likes physical interaction. He enjoys adventures and spontaneous activities. He has these raging hormones and a crying need for love and intimacy.

He might have been able to struggle on, controlling and channelling his appetites until marriage, if he was heterosexual. Teenage Christians are capable of tremendous commitment to Christ, and even enjoy the challenge of sacrifice. But the gay teenager has no such end in view. He is faced with tension and conflict building up that makes life near intolerable. Unless there is some move from the family, or the church, to show that they genuinely understand and are prepared to stand by him/her whatever, then he/she is highly likely to be lost to all evangelical church influence. They will probably reject much of their background and upbringing, and unless their parents are extremely careful and wise, they may reject their parents as well.

For a while they may hate all their parents represent, and that will affect their attitude towards the parents themselves. It won't help them for parents to keep telling how much they love them, if they keep following it by "but the Bible says". They will depart from the home, as quickly as they are free to do so, to the gay ghetto where they can develop an alternative lifestyle which seems to meet their situation. Of course they will have escaped one set of problems for another. But at least it will be their choice. I'm reminded again of Michael Vasey's quotation from the Episcopalian bishop William Swing; "We have homosexual ghettos as a memorial to families all over the USA who cannot deal with their homosexual children. Gay people differ from other cultural minorities in that they start their journey alone. It takes two straights to make a gay. In a society which has no positive or overt understanding of same sex sexual attraction, the journey starts in unnamed darkness and involves considerable pain".

Start With the Real, Work to the Ideal

What do parents do to avert this? The same as I do with all the practising gay people I counsel; I begin with the real, with the hope of working to something better.

Recently I applied for my ministerial credentials to be transferred from my church group in Britain to the same denomination in South Africa. Even though I am now a busy, but semi-retired, minister and not seeking a pastoral appointment, my application was turned down by the executive of the denomination. They accepted totally that I had never involved myself in homosexual acts, but they felt that my policy of 'starting with the real and working to the ideal' was a serious compromise of Biblical principles.

In fact pastors frequently do that in a variety of difficult situations; couples living together, marriage breakdowns, dealing with alcohol and other forms of addiction. But most evangelicals have decided that homosexuality is a sin in a category of its own. My quarrel with many evangelical churches is not because they have a negative view of homosexuality, but because they have no genuine pastoral understanding or concern for gay people.

My guess is that few of the executive members, who turned me down, seriously engage with practising homosexuals on a regular basis. Knowing the reception they are likely to receive, most gay people will avoid them. So like Pontius Pilate these leaders can 'wash their hands' and keep free from contamination. But my frequent contact with gay people tells me that unless I can learn to 'sit where they sit', love them unconditionally, and begin with the realities of what they struggle with, I have little hope of helping them. In all likelihood I will not see them again.

So parents, in my opinion, must begin there. It is right and proper for Christian parents to warn their children of the dangers of pursuing a homosexual lifestyle. It is right for them to share their insights into Scripture on the subject. It is right to pray earnestly for them. But the thing that the teenager needs more than anything else, at that point in their lives, is unconditional love and acceptance by their parents - to hear them say "You are my child, and I love you and accept you whatever. I will always listen to you and I will stand by you, and stand up for you, even when I disagree with you".

There is a time and place for so called 'tough love' but that isn't it. That, plus constant praying, is more likely to keep them in the safer environment of the home and the fellowship of a loving Christian church. The problems of dealing with homosexual desires and feelings is so great that, in my opinion, only the Holy Spirit can keep them from treading dangerous waters. I have never yet seen anyone give up pursuing a homosexual life-style as a result of condemnation, or by their own will power. The condemnation in fact tends to produce a 'bloody-mindedness' in the gay young person, that makes them rebel even more.

Only growth in personal faith and experience of God, backed by the loving understanding of the parents and family, makes it possible to avoid extremes. Even then there has to be a willingness, by the parents and church, to accept failure by the homosexual in his/her struggle. It is my firm view, as I've made clear already, that there is no cure. Reality tells me that those who are truly homosexual will always struggle. I've referred to a wife who has been able to keep her marriage together for more than twenty years by her ability to accept that her homosexual husband will fail sometimes, and her ability to love and forgive him when he does. That means a tremendous struggle for her as well as him. Parents must be prepared to pay that cost as well. And it must be a genuine acceptance, not a patronising one that robs the gay person of their dignity. People with low self-esteem are much more likely to turn to drugs, booze and sex to solve their problems.

Never Put Gay People out of the Family

I could tell you story after story of families who have treated their gay children scandalously, all in the name of being true to God and His Word. A few nights ago I heard a gay singer on TV tell an audience of young people," God is a cuddly toy for grownups. He doesn't actually exist". I was deeply disturbed by the comment and the venom beyond it. But the hatred felt against God by so many gay people is often a direct result of the hatred they have experienced through religious people, including some parents, all in the name of God. Every time I am faced with this, when I'm counselling gay people, I feel angry at what some evangelical Christians have done to cause this alienation between gay people and God.

Michael Vasey comments, "The Church can choose to put gay people out of its fellowship. But parents should NEVER put gay children out of the family". There is a very important distinction made in that statement. If a local church feels its principles and beliefs are being violated by one of its members, it is not only entitled to discipline or dis-fellowship the offender, it can claim Biblical support for doing so. The Christian parents of the offender, however, though they might agree with the church's principles, would not have same right to exclude their child from the family.

Why do Christian parents often handle their gay children so

badly? Earlier I said that all parents tend to indulge in an element of flagellation when their children fail. But this is particularly true with Christian parents when the failure is perceived to be moral or spiritual. Finding you have a gay child can be seen as both. "What did I do wrong?" Sometimes people raise that question when they give birth to a seriously handicapped child. But at least people now recognise the question to be illogical. The same is true for parents of gay children. If homosexuality is one of the many results of living in a fallen world, is mainly attributable to nature and not nurture, there is no logic in apportioning blame. But we don't always respond logically to difficult situations. I suspect that sometimes parents of gay children, who are torturing themselves over such questions, pass some of the blame for their feelings on to the child. They are thinking of their own need more than that of their son or daughter.

There are other variations of this self-centred attitude. Parents' dreams have been shattered. A macho dad, who has plans for his son sharing his own passion for football, has a mental picture of himself showing the ropes to his son, in the park. He looks forward to bragging about his son scoring a goal for the school first team, maybe has visions of a future Wayne Rooney in the family. Now he has a kid who other kids laugh at when it comes to sport. It's humiliating when he hears his son called a 'fag'. Can you imagine him going to the pub and telling his mates that he's proud of his 'gay son'. But Christian dads wouldn't be like that, you say. I'm not so sure.

I was surprised by a letter I saw in this week's local newspaper. It was from a member of my own church who I respect as a zealous Christian. He was angered by the local school head who had spoken out about some of the more negative aspects of competitiveness in school sport. Sport is a religion in South Africa. I thought the head had made some valid points; but my friend would have none of it. It showed me that sport stirs such passion in the male of the species that even Christians can be blinded by it. The female equivalent is what happens when mum assumes, because her son or daughter is gay, that she's never going to be able to organise a marriage ceremony or have grandchildren. Many people who are middle-aged, and older, try to deal with their own disappointments in life by living their lives through their children, and then their grand-children.

A further reason for parents reacting negatively to discovering their children are gay, is not so much their own feelings on the issue, but what others will say. "What will the people at the church think?" Some of the church folk may even raise the question of whether dad should still be an elder, for instance, in the light of 1 Timothy 3.

The pressure of the attitudes of 'the brothers' has been one of the more unlovely aspects of evangelical church life. Because so much of the social, as well as spiritual, life of the Christian family revolves around the local church, the opinion of others can be very important and determinative. Sad to say, it seems to be more important to some parents than what their gay children are going through. The pastor's attitude can be particularly important. We all want the approval of our pastor. In my experience, however, pastors are sometimes more homophobic than their congregations. Because they are public figures, who teach the sheep the right way to go, they are understandably concerned about making mistakes, or being seen as too lax. This can sometimes blind them to seeing things which folk in the congregation can see, because they have more contact with the real world.

Pastors and leaders are to be held in respect and honoured for the work they do, but they are not always right. We can honour them and at the same time disagree with them. A time can come when the parent of a gay teen may need to disagree with the pastor and the church, without undermining him or being disruptive in the church fellowship. Our children come before pastors. Christian parents who don't think for themselves, and allow all their attitudes to be shaped by the local church community, are going to find themselves increasingly in conflict with the non-Christians they work with and live amongst. Because it seems that society is ahead of the church, at the present time, in its ability to understand and be compassionate towards homosexuals.

In some households there is also a struggle for 'control'. Christian husbands who over-assert their 'headship', women who use their wiles to build a power base of their own. My dad was in most respects a strong man. But my mother almost always won in any dispute, because she used sanctions to get her way, especially by creating a 'blanket of silence' in the house. She was capable of 'sending us all to Coventry'. Parents sometimes do that with their children to make up for their lack of control in other areas of life. The power base they lack at work, or in the church, they try and build in the family.

Many parents try to hang on to control of their teenage children longer than they should. It's much harder to let go than we realise. I used to wonder why I found wedding rehearsals so stressful. Sometimes there was something akin to mayhem, everyone shouting their opinions on how things should be done. They took twice as long as they should have done. I observed that the main culprit was usually the bride's mother. Then I realised why. Instinctively she knows this is the last time she will have 'a right' to control something important in the life of her daughter.

Christian parents often try to force their children to go to church long after they have reached teens, and decided they don't want to go anymore. "While you live under my roof, and I pay the bills, you will do as I tell you" kind of attitude. Sanctions like that never really work, and they are wrong. But it's so hard to let go. "Didn't I make enormous sacrifice when you were small and sick? Hasn't it cost me a lot to bring you up? Don't I have the right to make these decisions?"

So when teenager emerges and adds the worst ingratitude, "Mum, Dad, I'm gay and I want to go to the gay teen club, and bring my gay friends home", the answer is obviously "How dare you try and corrupt my home by what is an abomination to God?" But it is still basically about us, and what we want for our kids' lives. True parenting and true love subordinates the need of the parent. You may even have to give that child more attention than others in the family. He doesn't need cosseting but he does need time and understanding.

Where Does a Parent Draw a Line?

But what if you get over this? You are loving, understanding, and supportive to your teenager in his/her struggles. But should you draw a line, and where do you draw it? The pastor has said, "Yes, I understand, you are homosexual by orientation. But you do realise it stops there?" Will it stop there and what do you do if it doesn't? For some it may stop there. Some are sufficiently strong spiritually to resist temptation. Some are far too timid and shy to take it any further, much as they might want to. They may even develop a meaningful relationship with someone of the opposite sex. Sometimes gay boys are more comfortable with girls. At least they don't have to be macho. Some girls like hanging out with gay guys, become what is known as a 'fag hag', because the guy is not always bragging about his exploits or trying to get them into bed. A friendship might even develop where they begin to consider the possibility of marriage.

The girl in fact falls in love with the guy, and then convinces herself that perhaps she can change him. He thinks that maybe it would be nice to have the comforts and respectability of marriage. In his own way he loves the girl, but it's not the kind of love needed for marriage. Parents should be very careful of encouraging it. Some real disasters take place through parents pushing in that direction. The fact that a person's 'balance of sexuality' makes it possible for them to have a sexual relationship with someone of the opposite sex, and that they have a genuine feeling of love towards the person, does not mean the marriage will work and solve the problem.

In a few cases, like one I've mentioned, it can be made to work. In most cases it doesn't work, and the couple lead separate lives or get divorced; and people get badly hurt, not least the heterosexual partner who has done nothing to deserve this. Marriage does not cure people of homosexual tendencies. Yet others simply 'fall into line', and somehow cope with being single. But there will always be the possibility, that those we think are coping, will one day meet someone and 'fall in love'. It happens like that, out of the blue, in exactly the same way as it does with heterosexual people.

The way in which it happens is the same, the symptoms are the same. Maybe this young Christian, who has a strong love for the Lord, has no desire for it to happen. He's coped for a number of years. But then one day 'Mr Right' comes along and 'Mr Right' makes the moves, comes on to him. And before he knows what's happening his whole world is changing, all those wonderful feelings come into play that every lover since creation has known. 'Mr Right' may also be a strong Christian, they may also be compatible in their outlook, their temperament, all the areas which we regard as important with heterosexuals who are thinking of a permanent relationship. They both agree that promiscuity is wrong, that getting involved in the 'gay scene' is not what they want. They agree that there is a lot of stuff out there which is unhealthy and very wrong. But they have no doubt they want to be with one another. And as their relationship develops, like any other couple in love they begin to express that love in physical ways. At first it's just kissing and cuddling. It may even stop there. But it will probably go beyond that. They start stopping over some nights, exploring the sexual side of their relationship but not going all the way. It may be a long time before they move in together. But eventually they do. They are now adults and they have the freedom to do so.

Their Christian families and friends may look on with pain and disappointment, expecting yet worse to happen. But all they see is two guys, or girls, setting up home together just as any other couple might do, because gay people have essentially the same goals as any one else. It's noticeable that when gays get into long term relationship they move out of the gay ghetto into the suburbs, into a nice neighbourhood. They buy a house. They go shopping a lot, looking for furnishings. Gay men in particular often have great taste in home design and decoration. The two lots of gay friends I stay with when visiting California have beautiful homes, immaculately kept. They want a nice garden, a dog, and even these days, children. One of the couples in California are about to adopt, something they have been planning for and preparing for a long time.

In other words gay couples become as domesticated as anyone else. By the time they are thirty, even if they have spent a lot of time in gay bars or clubbing in the past, they become thoroughly boring, just like their heterosexual neighbours, spending their evenings at home watching TV. Someone may point out that the long-term success rate of such partnerships is not good, especially with gay men. But it's not good with their heterosexual neighbours either, even Christian neighbours.

How should Christian parents react to such a scenario when it involves their children? They should do exactly the same as they do with their other children who have made their own choices in adulthood and moved in with a partner of the opposite sex. You get over it, get used to it, you welcome the partner into your home. Because if you don't, you know you are likely to lose regular contact with your children. In some respects you need them more than they need you. No parent has the right to insist that their children do only the things that they approve of. They have the absolute right to make their own choices.

When the adult daughter of a female friend of mine moved in with her boyfriend earlier than the mother was ready for, the mother was upset. But she realised that she would get nowhere going down that path. She welcomed the boyfriend into her home, and did it generously. If he stayed overnight she accepted they would sleep together; they were adults, not teenagers. That didn't mean approval, and the daughter knew it. It was an acceptance of reality. What it did do was enable her to get into the heart of this young man, and eventually lead him to Christ.

Having gay children, who have made their choices in life, choices of which you do not approve, does not mean you cannot have a good and meaningful relationship with them. Nor does it mean they have turned their backs on God. Bad attitudes on your part may cause them to turn their backs on God.

I have a Christian friend in California who is gay and has a partner. He is also a pastor of a church which he started, a church which reaches out to gay people with the Gospel and has quite a few practising gay people who are part of it. Such a situation is incomprehensible to most evangelical Christians and I understand that. His father is also an evangelical pastor of many years standing. I am sure his father has gone through a lot of pain over the path his son has chosen. I am sure he does not approve of homosexual practice. But when his son needs advice to help him in pastoring his church, he rings his father. They talk a lot on the phone, because they live at opposite ends of the country. I know his dad loves him, even as he loves his dad very much. I think the dad might even manage to be a little proud of him. He hasn't changed his own beliefs and principles, but this is his son and will always be his son and both of them enjoy the good relationship they have.

I have other friends, now in advanced years, who used to be missionaries. Over the last thirty years I have sat at their table for meals many, many times. They have several children; one of whom is gay. He has lived with his partner for perhaps twenty years. The partner has been there with the son at the table at family meals and always been treated as part of the family. The parents never talk about it; I doubt if they approve of it, but it has never once reflected in their attitudes. They love that son just as much as all their children; I'm sure they have developed a love for his partner, and they respect their right to make their own choices in life.

Chapter Eight - Where do we go from here?

There are no easy answers. Some painful things have happened to me in the months since I wrote the last chapter. It's more than two years since I returned to live in the city where I was first 'outed' as a gay man fifteen years ago. So I am known here, for who I am, more than anywhere else. But I also have a record here of planting and pastoring churches, some of which have been very successful. A good many people have come to know Christ through my ministry in this city. Apart from the one factor, of my sexual orientation, my record is untarnished. In the many discussions that take place in the press, on TV and in theological circles, it is invariably stated that sexual orientation is not in itself a bar to ministry. The necessity of celibacy is always the point at issue. Most denominations have affirmed this in resolutions and statements.

But I have discovered that this is not always how it works out. The refusal, some months ago, by the Baptist Union of South Africa, to accept transfer of my credentials from the Baptist Union of Great Britain, was not because of any suspicion concerning my sexual activities, but because of the kind of views I've expressed in this book. These views are regarded as 'revisionist' and unscriptural. Over the past year or two it has become apparent that the pulpits and platforms of a good many churches are closed to me because of my views; though in fact most of them have never heard my views.

I had an example not too long ago. I live in a small coastal town on the edge of the city, with about twenty churches mostly of an evangelical persuasion. Each year a united service is held on the beach the Sunday evening before Christmas. I've preached at that service a number of times in the past and I received an invitation from the committee of the ministers' fraternal to do so last year. As soon as it was announced that I was to be the speaker a number of ministers threatened to withdraw their congregations from participation if I was to speak. I solved the problem by standing down immediately.

The more moderate ministers, it seems, just capitulated to the conservative minority. But it was pointed out that most of the ministers had no direct or detailed knowledge of what I believe or what I am supposed to have 'done wrong'. So it was suggested I be asked to speak at the next meeting of the fraternal. I accepted. A number of these men are friends of past days and I looked forward to sharing with them. The chairman was a man very prominent in his denomination. I had in former years preached at the annual meetings of the churches over which he presided, for a whole week. I was honoured and praised by him for my ministry. But when I got to the ministers' fraternal meeting he didn't greet me, welcome me or even acknowledge he knew me. I was treated with considerable coldness and not as a brother.

Worst of all I discovered I had been allocated only 10-15 minutes to speak, instead of the 30-40 minutes I'd expected. It is impossible to deal with such a difficult and delicate issue in so short a time. But instead of protesting I decided to be humble. Looking back I think I was wrong. More harm than good is done by trying to compress such a controversial subject. I left feeling demeaned. It left me feeling very isolated in the town for a while. I was greeted coolly in the street by one or two church leaders.

Thank God there has been some change in the period since then. One pastor in particular, with a fairly large congregation, has invited me to preach for him regularly. And I have often known God's blessing on the preaching beyond the normal. It has not only restored my sense of self-worth but caused a change of attitude to me in the general community. Other things have happened in that time, in particular God's provision of a lovely new home that have caused people to comment on God's blessing on my life. I know that this in itself is causing some people to think again about this issue of homosexuality.

Clergy are the Main Problem

But all these recent happenings make me totally realistic about the obstacles there are in the way to change. I'm convinced that the main problem lies with ministers. Many lay-folk are waiting for a lead. Ministers hate admitting they may have been wrong and they often get intimidated by those who are homophobic. Evangelicals hate being thought 'unsound'. This is a crucial issue that I'm going to expand later. Unwittingly 'fear of the brothers' can make evangelical leaders more concerned to be thought 'sound' than to be seen as compassionate.

I've often wondered why so few of the members of that fraternal stuck out their necks for me. It made me realise that I was dispensable, because I am classified among a group of people who are shown scant sympathy by many evangelicals. Around that time I was also being harassed by a layman who called himself 'God's watchman in the valley' (the town's in a valley). He had previously spread rumours about other ministers and was doing it about me. Perhaps some of these ministers were worried that he, or some of the very conservative ministers, might mark them out as compromisers. But what they overlook is that there are many folk in their congregations looking for their pastors to take a lead. This is particularly true of the younger people. Young people in our churches are not impressed by dogma which appears to be inconsistent with the spirit of the Gospel. If leaders continue to be homophobic they will find young Christians leaving their churches.

A recent article in *The Economist* magazine, dealing with the strength and political influence of the 'Religious Right' in the

USA, commented that this over-involvement in right-wing politics by evangelical Christians was causing a reaction amongst the younger members of their churches. Numbers are beginning to drift away, not because they do not believe the evangelical message anymore, but because of the unbalanced and often harsh attitudes on important social issues; the poor, the environment, capital punishment and homosexuality. The American evangelical, Jim Wallis, who heads up the important Sojourners ministry in Washington D.C, writes in a recent book of the 'mean spiritedness' of much of the Religious Right to gay people.

Young people begin to sense that there has to be something fundamentally wrong with an outlook, and theology, that leads to such meanness. For good or bad, post-modern young people put Christian practice and life-style before dogma. There are some dangers in this. The end result may be that they get pushed too far in the opposite direction. There are areas where these young people need to be rooted more deeply in Biblical doctrines and values. They need, like their forefathers, 'to contend for the faith that was once entrusted to the saints' (Jude). But when it comes to compassion, and human values, many young people of today are way ahead of their elders.

Some of them absolutely shine. The rock-band leader Bono is a good example of this. He is not much enamoured by the church anymore, but his faith is real and his application of it to needy peoples of the world has been outstanding. There is far more respect for him from important political leaders, and certainly a great many Christian young people, than there is for even the best of evangelical church leaders. Thousands of young people, including church young people, have taken up his challenge and woken up their churches and governments to the needs of the world's millions of deprived and suffering. Those same young people have little time for the minutia of internal church politics and doctrinal debates. This is not going to change. We will have to find new ways of preserving the essentials of our doctrinal beliefs that make more sense to coming generations.   In fact a living, active church, empowered by the Holy Spirit has always been a greater protection against error than doctrinal formularies.

The Young do it Differently

I attended a wedding not long ago of two young people from conservative church homes.   One of them came from the traditionally very conservative South African Afrikaans community. The fathers of both were evangelical ministers. I'd got to know the bride's parents and sisters in recent years. I loved sharing in their meals because the conversation of the three daughters, husbands, boyfriend, and other Afrikaans-speaking young people who were often there, was so fresh, relevant and stimulating. The wedding service reflected this. The bride came down the aisle to a saxophone solo of "What a difference a day makes", rather than the usual Wagner or Mendelssohn.   The well-wishers blew bubbles instead of throwing confetti - and this was South Africa, not Hollywood.

The father of the bride brought a message in which he spoke of how often he'd worried about the unconventional ways his daughters expressed their faith as they grew up; how they refused just to slot into normal church ways of doing things. How they questioned traditional values before they took them on. But he went on to say that the more he had watched them in adult life the more it had made a profound impression on him. He described how whenever he visited the small flat of the bridal-daughter he would find a variety of folk there, some of whom he would have hesitated to have in his own home. He was amazed at how much she cared for these folk and their needs. It had, he said, opened his eyes to what the Christian faith is really about.

There's a whole generation of Christians out there who are bringing about changes for good in society, and in the church. I've described earlier how a hundred and fifty young people, members of a conservative church, applauded me loudly when I spoke of my experiences as a gay man, at their summer camp. Evangelical leaders will have to listen to these young people or they will find other ways of expressing their faith than in and through traditional church structures. We evangelicals are so sure that we understand the Christian faith better than others.

Philip Yancey in his *"The Jesus I never knew"*, resonated with me and helped me to realise that, by concentrating on the Epistles, many of us have never really understood the gospels or the Jesus of the gospels, the human Jesus. It's uncomfortable reading at times. One of the privileges of living in Africa is that one feels far nearer to the gospels in African village, or township, life than in the middle-class suburbs of Europe or America. The people Jesus felt most comfortable with were the people that evangelical westerners feel least comfortable with; and the people he felt very uncomfortable with sometimes looking remarkably like us - Pharisees, so orthodox, so correct, yet so lacking in compassion; so sure they are right that they are blind to see how very wrong they can actually be.

We do not know how Jesus regarded gay people or dealt with them. He must have met some. But whatever, I suspect that he treated them very differently from the way many conservative Christians have done. I heard on Sky news today that the Roman Catholic Primate in England is putting pressure on the British government to allow his church to discriminate against gay couples who want to adopt children from government-funded Catholic children's homes, because it violates Catholic moral teaching. No doubt there are some valid reasons for that. But it also tells me that even Cardinals wear blinkers when it comes to gays. They are seen as 'different' from normal, decent folk; not to be trusted with the welfare of children. It is an absurd, and highly prejudiced, caricature. I haven't come to final conclusions on the question of gay marriages; but I know quite a few gay couples who are doing an excellent job in bringing up children. Only religious bigotry, Pharisaism, could be blind enough not to see and know that.

But <u>Where</u> do we go from Here?

But I'm still not answering the question my friends are clamouring for me to answer. WHERE DO WE GO FROM HERE? Let me make some points that will clear the decks a little more, so we can come to some more practical suggestions.

We can begin by stating an obvious fact. Radical change is already upon us when it comes to governments and gay people, and the general public and gay people. European nations, in particular, have either changed or are in the process of changing laws in order to permit same sex partnerships, putting them on a level with heterosexual marriages. But it's not limited to Europe. In South Africa and in Massachusetts it is now possible for same sex couples to get married. And incidentally, contrary to all the dire predictions of the mayhem this would cause, there has been no stampede of people rushing to the altar in any of these situations. Life goes on very much as before; people adjust to it remarkably quickly and heterosexuals continue making a mess of their marriages without any help from gay people or any change in the law. But the public reaction in Britain was very much more than a resigned acceptance. It aroused enormous public interest. On the day when the first same-sex civil partnership ceremonies were performed there was considerable TV coverage.

There is no question that the high level of interest was accompanied by general public support. Only in Belfast was there a public protest and the fact that it was relatively low-key, in a province with a high concentration of conservative Christians, and where feeling often runs very high on religious issues, is in itself surprising. The partnership ceremony of the celebrity Sir Elton John and David Furnish was given several hours of coverage on TV and drew crowds in Windsor, where it took place, not dissimilar from those at the wedding of Prince Charles and Camilla Parker-Bowles a few months earlier. Both ceremonies were conducted by the same marriage officer in the same building.

Around the same time I had watched on TV the finals of the Strictly Come Dancing contest, a competition in which a professional dancer trains and is coupled with a public celebrity who has previously been unable to dance. One of the celebrities was Julian Clary, a very open and obvious gay man who is frequently in the public eye. His regular somewhat raunchy TV programme has had a large following amongst non-gay people. Julian was not one of the better dancers in the competition. The judges frequently gave him low marks. But he and his partner got as far as the final because the public telephone-voting constantly over-ruled the opinions of the judges. It is only a few years since it was suicidal for a politician to admit that he/she was gay. Now even prominent Conservative members of Parliament can 'come-out' with little or no difficulty. I've already recorded how in 2000 I stood out against almost all the evangelical ministers in the town in England where I was pastoring, when they protested at Tony Blair's proposals to repeal the anti-gay Section 28 legislation, which Mrs Thatcher introduced. It is now history. It was repealed with no difficulty, and with the support of a good many Conservative members of Parliament.

If I had had prophetic insight, and been able to tell that group of ministers in England that within two years Section 28 would be repealed with virtually no opposition, and within five years gay civil partnerships would be legalised, they would have regarded my prophecy as apocalyptic. I was attacked vigorously in the local press by evangelical Christians. How tame it all seems to most people now. A prominent Conservative politician interviewed on TV was asked whether he thought there could ever be a leader of the Conservative party who was openly gay. He replied in the affirmative.

What have Changes in Society got to do with the Church?

Evangelical Christians will say, of course, that all this has no relevance to what the church believes and does. That is manifestly not true. We do not practise our faith in a vacuum, but in a real world in which the people of the world's eyes are often very critically upon us. Individual Christians, and churches, have changed their views on a good many issues as a result of changes in society. Churches are still working through the impact on them of changes in society over the role of women. It has already caused ecclesiastical splits. Only the most conservative groups have been able to resist the pressure to allow women the same positions as men in church life and structures.

The churches which have changed will argue that they have now come to a better understanding of Scripture. But there is little question that the changes did not begin as a result of this 'new theological light'. They began through women (and men) in the churches, who saw the changes in society, and were no longer willing to be treated to what they regarded as 'second-class citizenship in the Church'. For much of my life and ministry I have been involved with churches that believe that Scripture teaches headship is male, and still believe and practise that. But from my contact with lay folk in those churches I know that there are many who are deeply unhappy about this. Whilst not abandoning their belief in male headship, nearly all these churches have had to find ways of accommodating the genuine aspirations of women members, in ways they would not have accepted a generation ago.

For good or ill we are influenced more than we like to admit by the changes in the world around us. We may decide to stand our ground, and ignore what the world thinks and says, but we will pay the price of being seen as irrelevant as well as bigoted. I'm reminded of the joke about the nineteenth-century bishop's wife, who when told of Darwin's theory that man is descended from the ape, said "Let's pray that it's not true. And if it is true that it may not become generally known". The church in Britain has already had to pay a very high price for its apparent irrelevance.

There will continue to be many who will resist Change

Having said all that, my second projection is that there will continue to be a considerable body of conservative Christians who will continue to resist change. They may even be the majority, though not in the long run. Most will be people of sincere conviction who have no desire to be gay-bashers or bigots. I have often been on the conservative side in theological arguments and debates. It is never pleasant when Christians feel they have to divide. In fact it is a tragedy. But I cannot criticise conservative Christians who stand their ground on matters of principle when I have done the same myself.

Forty years ago I resigned from the denominational group to which I then belonged when it elected as President a man who denied the deity of Christ. Only a few years ago I vigorously opposed an invitation to the head of the Roman Catholic Church in Britain to speak at the main annual gathering of the churches of my denomination. I was virtually on my own in opposition, but for me it was a matter of conscience, even if everyone else thought I was Neanderthal man. It is not tragic when people stand up for what they believe. Where would the Christian church have been without them? What would have happened if Martin Luther had not taken his stand for "Justification through faith alone". What would have happened if John Wesley had given in to pressure from Anglican bishops and ceased to preach the gospel in the highways and byways of England, even though it led eventually to a split in the Anglican Church? What is tragic is when Christians malign fellow believers, deny they are part of the body of Christ, or exaggerate what they say or do from sincere conviction. This is particularly so when the issues involved, though very important, are not fundamental to the Gospel.

In the homosexual debate there is a particular dividing line which makes it, in my opinion, virtually impossible for Christians to move forward together at the present time. It is the dividing line between those who believe that the overwhelming evidence is that homosexual orientation is a result of nature more than nurture, and those who take the opposite view. Those who put all the emphasis on nurture believe that therefore the homosexual condition is a matter of choice. Which means the condition can be reversed. Evangelical Christians, because of the understandable fears they have about negative changes in the church and in society, have a tendency to take up extreme positions. So, sadly, we are often seen as reactive rather than proactive.

One example is in the current debate about abortion. Whilst almost all Christians are horrified at the unwarranted slaughter of babies at the present time, some pro-lifers go too far and so harm their cause. Some pastors I know do the same with divorce, refusing ever to re-marry divorcees whatever the reason for the divorce. I believe that some Christians, in rejecting the philosophy of evolution that has often accompanied the theory of evolution, go too far in refusing to recognise any truth in the scientific theory of evolution. There are some evangelicals who will continue to dig yet deeper ditches in their opposition to any concessions to gay people. They will try and make any change impossible in their churches by threatening secession. Those who want change, and believe that change must come because the Gospel requires it, may have to be willing to let them go. Unity can sometimes be bought at too high a price. As we've seen John Wesley unintentionally split the Anglican Church by his preaching of the Gospel. Christians in the USA were split by the issue of slavery.

One of the things we need to recognise is that not all the opposition is theological, though it is clothed in theological terms. I've written more than once about the power of homophobia. A recognition of this is key to any progress. In my conversations with leaders I frequently plead with them to be honest about their feelings; because like any form of wrong prejudice, it has a tendency to distort and blind. But there is also the question of culture.

We sometimes confuse conservative culture with Christian

193

morality. The Anglican Church world-wide faces what appears to be an insoluble situation over homosexuality. The fissures of a split, more serious than anything in recent history, are widening daily, bigger than that over the ordination of women. One of the things that make it appear insoluble is the opposition to any change from many of the large communities of evangelicals amongst Anglicans in Africa and Asia. They may even represent the majority of Anglican members world-wide.

The Ordination of Practising Gay Clergy & Bishops

I do not support the position of liberal Anglican Church leaders in the western world. If I were an Anglican I would not support the ordination of practising gay clergy, even less bishops. That will upset some of my gay readers. But I believe it is part of the sacrifice that gay people, who want to see change, have to make. When it comes to leadership, standards are sometimes required that are not insisted upon for ordinary church members. For years divorced people were not appointed to leadership positions, whether as ordained clergy in some denominations, or elders in others. Gradually changes were made where potential leaders were seen to be the innocent party in a marriage break-up. But I still think a person should not put himself forward for public office, in the church, if he has been through a number of such break-ups.

The most influential evangelical leader in South Africa seriously harmed his ministry a few years ago by divorcing his wife, for unconvincing reasons, and then married a younger woman a few months later. He continued to minister, and effectively, but he lost completely the strategic influence he had in the nation; because he lost respect. *Gay Christians have to recognise the church is not ready, if it ever will be, for practising gay people to be in charge of churches.* No serious Christian would want to create division and bring leadership into disrepute. For me personally, if I should, for whatever reason, abandon my celibacy as a gay man, I would feel it necessary to step down from any leadership position I held. Because the path ahead is not clear, and much is at stake, Christians who are gay should be willing for some sacrifice.

But just as I do not accept the position of many liberal church leaders, nor do I agree with aspects of the opposition to change from conservative church leaders. This is particularly true of church leaders in the so-called third world (now a misnomer) who feature so much in the present debate. Recently when my transfer of accreditation was refused by the executive of the Baptist Union of South Africa, because I am an openly gay man, the official reason given in writing was my 'bad hermeneutics'; i.e. my querying of the traditional interpretation of some of the Scriptures which refer to homosexuality. By doing that they have put themselves in an indefensible position. But they also told me what I am sure is the bigger reason; the opposition they expected from the black leaders of the denomination.

Though I believe the mainly white executive acted in a cowardly fashion that will rebound on them, I understand their fear. Having worked with black churches and leaders for more than a dozen years I know how deeply hostile their culture and traditions are to homosexuality. Some would claim this as evidence that homosexuality is a western perversion that doesn't exist in other cultures of the world. This is simply not true, as I have illustrated earlier. In multi-cultural gay gatherings there are always considerable representations of non-Caucasian people, including Africans. I am not criticising my African Christian brothers. I have found more faith, and passion, and love amongst them than any other group of people - sometimes by far. At the present time I am missing, badly, the congregation of black students to which I preached regularly until two years ago.

A recent trip back to Zambia, to visit my spiritual children from earlier years, was an overwhelming experience. I fought against apartheid in South Africa and all the racial evils it represented. Africa has become the centre of much of the world's concern and attention in recent years. But it saddens me that the concern is often based on pity rather than appreciation of the peoples of Africa. Most see Africa as a disease ridden, corrupt, economically bankrupt continent. So often this view is not balanced by an appreciation of the tremendous qualities of African people; the quality of family life, the quality of care for one another, their openness and friendship, their cheerfulness and joy often in the face of much adversity. But I am also not blind to the faults. Women are still often treated very badly. The macho image of the male is an enormous obstacle in bringing about needed changes.

African Views of Rape

I've recently done some research on the AIDS pandemic in the region in which I live. The church of which I am a member has an amazing ministry amongst HIV+ victims. The biggest hindrance in reducing the numbers dying, in my opinion, is the difficulty of getting people tested for HIV. Without that they will not get the treatments that can save their lives. With men the macho factor is a great hindrance to both use of condoms and getting tested. With women it is fear of what men may do to them if they are discovered to be HIV+. I've pointed out that in the case of women and children, who make up two-thirds of those known to be infected, the majority of them are not guilty of any great sin. They have been raped, or infected by their husbands, or forced into prostitution through poverty.

I've discussed it, debated it, with educated African evangelical leaders. But they have always refused my contention on this matter of guilt. Only recently did I finally realise why. When it comes to rape, very unlike the present situation in the western world, the women who get raped are almost always seen as 'having asked for it'. I think I will never understand African thinking and culture when it comes to sex. In many respects it reflects the religion of the Old Testament where women sometimes got a raw deal when they sinned. But that has no place under the New Covenant, as Jesus exemplified in the way he treated the woman who had been involved in adultery.

What am I saying? That the same kind of cultural factors that produce this attitude to women also come into play when it comes to gay people. I thank God that so many African church leaders are faithful to the Biblical Gospel and preach it with power and to much effect. I thank God when they resist a 'liberal Gospel' and stand up to western church leaders who have often dictated policies because they held the purse strings. I could record some shocking incidents I have witnessed of the latter. But I think that those of us who do not share the liberal theology of many western church leaders, and who love the African churches and their leaders, need to be careful in following their lead when it comes to homosexuality, as well as women's issues. More than theology is involved in their attitudes.

Change can start at Grass Roots

So, in trying to predict the future, it seems clear to me that evangelical Christians are not going to be able to move forward together on this one, anymore than they have been with a lot of other issues. That makes it particularly difficult in theologically mixed denominations where there is strong central government. In South Africa where the traditionally conservative Dutch Reformed Church is trying to escape from its apartheid past and identify with the new South Africa, that denomination has expressed its approval of the recent legalising of gay marriages. Sensibly they recognise it is a civil issue, not a church issue. But it is having great difficulty in giving answers to questions its congregants are calling for when it comes to gays within the church.

Although the really big issues may not be soluble at the present time, there is a lot of scope for change at local church level, especially in those church groups where government is less centralised. Tony Campolo refers to a growing number of local congregations, in his particular Baptist Convention, which are open to and affirming of gay people. Jim Wallis refers to a similar situation with main-stream Presbyterian churches in America. Change at the top often comes about best when it has risen from grass roots level. It would be so easy for congregations, who are concerned to be more open and compassionate, to shift the blame to top leadership when there is so much they could be doing without breaking any rules.

This evening, after typing this paragraph I went out to eat at my usual restaurant. It's a place that caters for traditional and mainly older people, in a conservative town with a large number of evangelical Christians. A white middle-class family, covering three generations, was sitting at the next table. They were discussing a gay wedding some of them had just been to - one of the first since the law changed. The mother said she had never heard vows as beautiful as those that had been made between the two men. Everyone seemed to agree that it was good that two guys, who had been together for eight years, should now be able to make it formal and legal. That's typical grass roots opinion, even in conservative places, at the present time.

The churches will have to take cognisance of it unless they are to be written off as uncaring and irrelevant. Earlier in the day a fine 40 year old Christian lady, who has been through Bible school, knows her Bible and theology, is a member of an evangelical church and involved in quite a few Christian activities in the town, came to help me with my computer. I told her the subject of this book. She immediately expressed approval and said that the churches had to wake up to the real situation. She commented "If only some of these folk knew some of the gay couples I know they would think differently". Again, typical grass-roots opinion even amongst committed Christian folk. Many evangelical lay folk have already gone a long way in forming their own opinions, without any positive help or guidance from their churches. Some leaders will finally speak up when it is already too late to affect the direction of things.

It Takes Two to Tango

It needs to be said at this point that change needs to come from both sides. Some of the gay Christian folk I talk with are actually themselves a hindrance to meaningful change because they 'demand the moon' and want it 'now'. Because they have waited so long to see change and find full acceptance, and sometimes suffered a lot, they lose patience. They need to understand that there are good reasons why evangelical churches find it harder to be accommodating than those of a more liberal theological outlook.

If you believe there are many interpretations of the Christian faith which are equally valid, then you have no difficulty in accepting one more. But for those who believe that there is a "Faith once for all entrusted to the saints", that we are called to contend for, it is much more difficult to accept change. We must weigh every change proposed very carefully. If there is only one Gospel, one Saviour and one way of salvation, then we must all - gay and straight - be concerned to preserve the uniqueness and clarity of that message. If the Gospel message is relative and changeable, then we can have no certainty of salvation for ourselves, or a certain hope to offer to others.

There must be no confusion amongst gay people. Those of us who are Christians are Christians first. That must be clear and visible in all we do and say. We should not desire any solution which requires a 'bending of the rules' to suit us. Acceptance of gay Christians as full members of the church family, and genuine compassion for those who are not yet family, must come about because it is part of the Gospel message and not a violation of it. Evangelical church leaders are right to be careful, and weigh the issues, before making big changes. Because we are Christians first, those of us who are gay should support them and respect them in doing it. It will mean a lot more patience and love on our part. We may well be treated with contempt by other gay people. Gay periodicals frequently scorn gay people who still persist with their adherence to the Christian church and the Gospel. *But in the end this is the way we will win, because it is the way of Christ's Cross.* The best changes always come with a degree of adversity and suffering.

Moving at the Right Speed

Recently I spent several hours with a couple visiting from a neighbouring country. They were once members of a church I pastored. They came to talk about a close relative who was also in that congregation. I have referred to her earlier in the book, a doctor who is a strong Christian and has been very faithful, but has struggled to maintain her fellowship with evangelical churches because she is a practising Lesbian. For many years she struggled to be celibate but eventually the struggle became too much. She is now in a long-term partnership with another Christian woman.

She is also pregnant through sperm donation. A high proportion of gay women long to have children just like any other woman, but find it impossible to do so by the normal means. Because of this she was recently asked to leave an evangelical church, just as she had been asked to leave two others before that. She is happy in her new family life, after years of struggle and pain. Even though she has been hurt so much by churches, acting as they did because they thought they were acting according to Scripture teaching, she still desires to be part of evangelical church life. She wants to hear the Gospel preached fully and faithfully, she wants to be taught from the Scriptures, she wants true spiritual worship and fellowship. The husband, of the couple who had come to talk with me, is an elder of that church. The lesbian is his sister in law, but also a close friend from before his marriage. He finds it difficult to accept the choices she has made but has a genuine love and concern for her, her partner and the child to be. He and his wife wanted to hear from me what I thought he should do.

There is no easy answer for an evangelical Christian who knows the realities of evangelical church life and thought. But because the woman has turned to me in her pain on a number of occasions over the years, because I have seen her pain, the agonising she has gone through in making her choices, because I have read her heart and seen her genuine love for Christ, I am in no doubt that I should support her. I do not know to what degree she might be in the wrong, but I know she is a sister and I know she needs my love and support. I don't have to agree with her a hundred per cent to stand by her. I urged the couple to take the same attitude. Other friends have suggested they 'hit her round the head with Bible verses' and shock her into recanting her ways! They accepted my advice that this was both wrong and wouldn't achieve anything positive. But there was still the concern of what will happen if she, her partner and child, start to attend the church of which he is an elder.

I urged him to do two things. First to talk with his fellow elders and get them to determine where they feel the boundaries are for them. I may not agree with what they decide but I recognise their right and responsibility as local church elders to do that. I know this particular elder to be a truly godly and compassionate man. They may well draw a boundary that excludes this 'gay family' from formal membership or active involvement in ministry, because they are a church with very clear and definite views. But I urged that in their decisions and attitudes they could not do less than accept and embrace this family as Christian people, with no equivocation or half-heartedness, and do nothing to embarrass them or prevent them getting spiritual food and fellowship through that church body.

But I also suggested to them that they should urge this relative, as family and friends, not to push for more than the elders were ready for, thereby inviting rejection and maybe possibility of further progress. It would also only add yet more hurt. On a previous occasion, in another evangelical church, she had asked for membership and the possibility of becoming a house group leader, which she had been good at in earlier years. She had been refused. Not many conservative churches are yet ready for that. Moving at the right speed is going to be crucial for bringing change in the more conservative of churches. Pushing it too hard would probably harm future progress.

I have already mentioned a lady in one of my churches 'who came out'. She was a member in very good standing, well respected and liked in the church. I am sure the leaders had no thought of putting her out of membership even though she had already entered into a relationship. But she asked for a letter from the elders stating that she and her partner were welcome at the Lord's Table. I know the elders had no intention of turning them away, particularly as we practised a table open to all believers. But to give her the letter she wanted would have implied more than the elders felt ready for. I urged her not to ask for too much, to accept my assurance that she and her partner would not be rejected or embarrassed in any way. I knew in fact that most of the leaders would go out of their way to make them feel at ease.

But I think she was determined to 'fly a flag', and she never came to the church again. I kept contact with her, and I understood why she did it, but I think gay Christians need to respond positively wherever Evangelical Church leaders seek to show a loving and compassionate attitude, and respect them where they have convictions which prevent them moving further at the particular time. This cautiousness on my part will distress, even anger, some of my gay readers. But there is so much to be gained by patience, and so much to be lost if gay Christians push too hard too soon.

Alright, preaching over! Let's get down to some more practical steps for those wanting to bring about change in their local situation.

1. Attitude

First, it all begins with attitudes; all change does. Romans 12:1-2 tells us "Do not conform any longer to the pattern of the world, but be transformed by the renewing of your mind. Then

you will be able to test and approve what God's will is....".
Homophobia is worldly, as is racism or sexism. It's 'natural' and
so we tend to think it's OK. But it comes from worldly thinking,
and dark feelings that come up from our inward fallenness. We
need to change our thinking not only about homosexuals as
people; but non-homosexuals who disagree with us on this
subject.

Tony Campolo in his book *"Speaking my Mind"* writes 'What
makes matters worse is that on each side of the argument
people demonise those on the other side.....We must not allow
ourselves to think that those who differ with us on the matter of
homosexuality are less Christian or even less committed to
Scripture than we are." I've discovered that quite a few of
those evangelicals who have difficulty with my views, and some
of them have been strong friends of mine, have in more recent
years written me off as backslidden. The fact that I went to
America to work with a 'gay church' proves it, they think. I've
told already how a friend and colleague preached a sermon in
which he clearly inferred that I had not gone to America as a
missionary to the gay community, but went looking for a
partner. But then they meet me face to face, hear me preach
(probably unintentionally) and find I'm the same Graham Ingram
that they knew years ago, I still love Jesus and still preach the
Gospel.

Open your mind to the possibility that you might not be totally
right in your present thinking. Read some books written from
the gay side, and not just from people who believe that gay
people can be 'delivered'. Be suspicious of people who have
simplistic interpretations or solutions. In his book Tony
Campolo writes "The reason most evangelicals want to believe
that homosexuals can change is because they are usually
convinced that to have homosexual orientation is to be
perverted......Insensitive preachers, trying to be cute in their
sermons, sometimes attempt to elicit a cheap laugh by saying
'God created Adam and Eve, not Adam and Steve".

I have pointed out earlier that it is much more complicated than that. It is not good enough to say that God would never have created people gay. You also have to ask, if that is your approach, 'Did God create people legless, or with two heads (which I've seen) or any of the multitude of deformities that have beset countless people from the time of birth'? We live in a fallen world and there are not simplistic answers or solutions. It will help you also if, instead of fearing, or avoiding, gay people you make a deliberate effort to get to know them. Ask them to tell you their stories. Most of them are willing.

I am confident of one thing in what I am saying. Any of you who do what I am suggesting, even if at the end of the day you do not change your understanding of Scripture, or your church policies in dealing with gay people, you will think of gay people very differently. And you will be the better for that and it will be a definite step forward for you.

2. Judgments based on Extremes

Secondly, don't make judgements based on extremes. Earlier in the chapter I referred to the fine qualities of many of the young people of the present generation, qualities that puts them ahead of many of their seniors. But many people in Europe today have a very different opinion of young people.

In Britain the Blair government has introduced policy after policy trying to deal with yobbo culture. Violence at international football matches has become a national disgrace. My nephew, in a recent e-mail, complained bitterly of the theft and thuggery experienced almost daily on his housing estate in the north of England. It is young people who were responsible for the loss of many lives in central London in recent years, through acts of terrorism. Some people just take hold of all these incidents and describe this generation of young people as if they were the worst ever.

There are frequent warnings of how important to is not to judge the Muslim community as a whole by a few who commit acts of violence. Muslim young people speak of how they feel picked on by the police, and looked at with suspicion by the general public, because of the colour of their skin, their dress or other indications of their culture or religion.

It's the same when it comes to gay people. A minority of gay people, especially males, are very promiscuous. Some who take part in Gay Pride parades, which often get major coverage on TV, are very 'in your face' in their slogans and in exhibiting their sexuality. It has been normal in films and TV sitcoms to portray gay people with limp wrists, hip wiggles, high-pitched voices and a whole lot of other things which give people a good laugh, but often rob the gay community as a whole of self-respect.

I was sickened a couple of nights ago in watching the BBC series "Cutting It" by the portrayal of the gay hairdresser. Few could respect such a weak, spineless individual. You probably know a few people who fit those descriptions and in your mind have that image of what it means to be gay. But you know a lot more people than you realise who are gay. You have just never recognised them. One is your doctor, another is a teacher in your son's school. One is a deacon or elder in your church. Those two old ladies who sit together in your church are gay and have been in love with each other for twenty years. Uncle Bert is gay, and your neighbour who is married is gay and struggles everyday in his/her life with what is still a strong temptation. Some of the gay couples you know are more upright, hardworking, decent, honest - even spiritual - than the great majority of folk around you.

The only difference, and the thing by which you judge them, is their sexual orientation, and the fact they feel they have to have someone to love. You have got to start seeing people as individuals, and judge them as such. One of the things that black people, especially here in South Africa, hate is that when a white person is mad with a black person, he will often say "You people always....etc,etc". He/she is not treated as an individual, but part of a whole mass of people who all have the same characteristics. Gay people are often treated in the same way.

3. Read the Gospels

Thirdly, when you are thinking about what Scripture teaches, don't just read about Sodom, or the verses in Leviticus or 1 Corinthians. Read the Gospels again, slowly, observing very carefully Jesus' attitude to people and his handling of people, people of all kinds, bad and good. Try and look at people through Jesus' eyes.

Think of what Paul says in 2 Corinthians 5:16 "From now on we regard no one from a worldly point of view. Though we once regarded Christ in this way, we do so no longer". He, like many others, had once seen Jesus through human eyes only and judged him to be a blasphemer. The Pharisees judged him as a 'glutton and a drunkard, and a Sabbath breaker', a thoroughly bad lot through their eyes and by their standards. That's what they 'saw', and therefore that's what they came to believe. They had been so totally wrong, and so had Paul. But he had had his eyes opened and now through the same eyes he had a completely different view of the world and of people. And now he was an altogether more compassionate man. Incidentally, all the people described in the Bible as homosexual are wicked people with no thought of God or care for God. Most of the gay people around you are not like that. That should make you think about how you apply the Scripture verses.

Again, consider the possibility that the issue may not be nearly as clear and straightforward as you have thought it to be.

Consider that Scripture, and your interpretation of it, is not so clear as you thought. Ministers and preachers find it difficult to accept that we may have got things wrong in the past. But we do change our views on other things in Scripture. In particular we don't like being asked to change from what we always thought was clear, for a position that seems full of questions and uncertainties. But every pioneer and explorer has had to do that. I do not want to put the treatment of homosexuals on a par with the treatment of slaves in the past, as some pro-gay writers have done. But I do think it needs to be pointed out that many slave owners in the American south were devout Christians and were blind to how serious their wrongdoing was.

This was equally true in South Africa until quite recent years. Afrikaners, in particular, were God-fearing people who really thought they were carrying out God's plan in the apartheid structures of society. The recent death of P.W. Botha, the last of the old-style apartheid Presidents, is an illustration of this. His funeral service was amazing. It was thoroughly evangelical in its content and tone. A Lebanese evangelist, who Botha had befriended in his latter years, preached a powerful evangelistic sermon and pleaded with people to commit themselves to Christ. Where else in the world would you get that at a State funeral?

Authentic testimonies, as well as the message from the pastor of the church, confirmed that Botha was a genuine born-again Christian. But to the end of his life Botha refused to change his attitude on his apartheid policies and found it very difficult to forgive the Dutch Reformed Church for 'repenting' of supporting apartheid. Many young Afrikaners have had real difficulty in coping with their shame about their past, including some of the children and grandchildren of the apartheid Prime Ministers who first instigated those policies.

Again, I say that there is not a direct parallel with the treatment of homosexuality. But we do need to consider the possibility that we have been wrong because wrong perceptions have blinded us. The issue is not as clear, as we long thought it to be, because Scripture in fact says nothing about gay people who were born with a same-sex orientation, and who love and fear God. So there is a real possibility that the Christian Church has treated many gay people shamefully in the past. Surely that must make all of us pause and re-consider in case we find ourselves on the opposite side from God.

Let me ask a big question. Do you want to change your attitude and practice, if Scripture will allow you to do so? Do you want at least to be much more compassionate? If you do, you will find ways of doing it. Don't look for excuses for maintaining your past position, because your reasons are likely to be very questionable.

4. Watch Your Words & Attitudes

If you really do want to move forward with change, you will need to watch your words and attitudes very carefully. One of the biggest mistakes that ministers and preachers make is to make the assumption that there are no homosexual people in their congregations; at least that is how most of them preach when it comes to this subject. I've mentioned earlier a young man who I tried to persuade to 'come out' to his pastor. His pastor had asked me to speak on the subject at a Sunday service just because he wanted to lead the church in new directions. I assured the young man that his pastor was a changed man. "Then why did he mimic a gay man carrying a hand-bag in a recent sermon"? That is unforgivable.

Every evangelical church leader, who is concerned for change must speak and act knowing that gay people will be listening to him and watching him. Even if he regards homosexual acts as wrong he must always speak of the dilemma of gay people with compassion, never as if he was judging them. Don't expect gay people to be ashamed of, or apologise for, who they are. They are not 'the black sheep' of God's family.

One of the silliest things that has happened to me was when one of my minister friends berated me for not being ashamed of being gay. I have never known what it means to be anything else and I feel comfortable with myself. I try and talk about my sexuality in a natural kind of way. If I don't speak about it, it is out of concern that others are going to be embarrassed, not that I am. It is not healthy for any Christian, or any person, to go through life carrying a burden of guilt on their shoulders for something they are not responsible for.

5. Don't Treat Gay People Differently

Treat gay people just like any other people. If you don't, you will never win them. I once made a bad mistake in a church of which I was pastor. I was still 'in the closet' myself but I was eager that the church should be reaching out to gay people. We were the kind of church which in its style, and its large congregation, had more chance of reaching gay people than most churches. We also had a number of members involved in the theatre and arts, where there tend to be a good many gay folk. So I was very pleased, but not over surprised, when I saw a group of folk come into one of our services who I recognised as being gay. Foolishly I made far too much of a fuss of them and made some stupid comment about how 'glad we are to have folk like you, and we want you to know that we love you'. They never came again.

One of the things that makes me very sad is that sometimes I get the feeling that evangelical Christians are more concerned to get gay people to 'change their wicked ways' than to win them for Christ. So they 'hit them with law' before showing any love or grace, and that only comes if they respond to being hit by the law.

Let me say to folk who reject my views as being too accommodating; *you are more likely to bring gay people to the life-style that you feel to be legitimate for a Christian, if you accept them and love them first.*

The daughter of a Christian friend of mine moved in with her boyfriend who was not a Christian. It was clearly a sexual relationship. Though my friend was unhappy about this, and no doubt she let her daughter know that, she decided to accept and love him unconditionally. The boy knew my friend's views on marriage. He was so impressed at the way she treated him that one day she was able to lead him to Christ, in her own home, and subsequently to marriage.

I've mentioned a minister friend of mine who had been actively gay when he was young. After his conversion he went through one of the ex-gay courses and subsequently became a minister and for a number of years was able to be celibate. He even considered heterosexual marriage. He contacted me one day and asked if I would visit him. He was in considerable distress. He was working under another minister who he felt had given him a very hard time. He had sought redress from the 'overseeing' minister of that group of churches, but he had shown little sympathy and more or less dismissed him as a 'no-good'. He was living in a city where he didn't know many people and was lonely. At the gym he met a gay man, who was also a Christian, who was attracted to him. By the time I heeded my friend's call for help he was already in a relationship. He'd managed to maintain celibacy until his life began to fall apart, and then he did what the alcoholic tends to do when he is miserable.

When the church discovered what was happening they did not handle it well or treat him well. He lost his job and eventually lost his home and for a period his 'sanity'. I've been in contact with him recently. He has regained his health, but I doubt very much whether he is ready to attempt celibacy yet. He has been devastated by how Christians have treated him. I'm sure he feels the need for someone to love him and accept him unconditionally. He has Christian friends who love him and accept him, but it is not the same as having a 'partner'. None of us can function well in life if we feel rejected and have low self-esteem, as a great many gay people have. Using 'the stick' virtually never produces the desired result.

6. Stick Your Neck Out

Six - Churches which are serious about making gay people feel welcome are also going to have to 'stick their neck' out on behalf of gay people. When in 1976 I moved to South Africa, to pastor a white church, I was determined to lead that church into being more truly representative of the racial mix of the area in which we lived. I convinced most of the existing members that this was right, but it was much harder to overcome the suspicions of other race groups. Occasional joint prayer meetings, or evangelistic services, with coloured and black churches, didn't do it. The folk who weren't white made it very clear that social acceptance was what they were looking for. And in the apartheid structures of South Africa that sometimes meant breaking the law.

It was by sticking our necks out on political issues, and even being willing to antagonise fellow white Christians, that we proved our sincerity and gained people. It is the same with any approach to gay people. Tony Campolo comments, "I sincerely hope that all Christians, regardless of their opinions about causes and possible 'cures' for homosexual orientations, will agree on at least this; homosexuals are entitled to the same civil rights that heterosexuals enjoy. We should not allow discrimination in the workplace or residential housing. If employers are willing to provide medical coverage for heterosexual couples living together out of wedlock then they must be ready to provide the same benefits for homosexual couples. The law should protect all citizens against hate crimes".

Most of these provisions now apply in 'western' societies but it is surprising how Christians are often amongst those who resent these provisions; they see it as 'undermining family values'. They should be ashamed. Campolo goes on "Unless heterosexual Christians are willing to champion calls for justice for gays and lesbians, it will be just about impossible to declare that the church loves them". I would add championing the cause of some form of gay 'marriage' or commitment ceremony, as coming in the same category. Evangelicals get so confused here. Championing the 'right' of gay people to have such a ceremony does not necessarily imply approval, or commit the church to being involved in such ceremonies. Marriage is a civil ceremony as well as a religious one.

Marriage is a Creation ordinance, for all people, not specifically Christian. On the continent of Europe the civil and the religious are normally separated. In the United Kingdom most people now have only a civil ceremony. That it is, in my opinion, better than the old days when people went hypocritically through a church ceremony as a tradition, making vows before God that they had little intention of keeping. Gay people have a right to the same civil provisions as anyone else, particularly when you accept that this is the only kind of 'marriage' commitment that most gay people are capable of making. It is simply a matter of justice that Christians should support this and the Bible, particularly the Old Testament, is very strong on the importance of justice to God.

7. Don't Expect Change Overnight

My seventh point - don't demand or expect gay folk, who have been involved in a gay lifestyle for years, to change overnight and adopt a completely different lifestyle. Even if they have a radical conversion, that leads to a lot of immediate change, it will probably not stay like that.

Tony Campolo is one of the few really well known evangelical leaders who has spoken up for the gay community; his wife even more so. He comments "I personally know many Christians with homosexual orientations who fight against their desires for homosexual behaviour through the power of the Holy Spirit. The desire to experience sexual gratification through physical involvement with persons of their own sex is a constant (just as heterosexual desire can be a constant) for many of them, but they are more than conquerors through Christ who strengthens them. I cannot help but admire these brave saints who endure lives of sexual frustration because of their commitment to what they believe are Biblical admonitions against homosexual eroticism. Many such Christians have told me about their long nights of spiritual agony, as they have struggled against the flesh to remain faithful to what they are sure is the will of God. Any who believe that these homosexuals who remain celibate for the sake of Christ are anything less than glorious victors in God's kingdom ought to be ashamed of themselves".

I am very grateful to Tony for sticking his neck out for gay people, because many other evangelicals in the States have punished him for it. But I am nonetheless somewhat irritated by aspects of that statement. Only a heterosexual man could make it. Giving me accolades, almost canonisation, doesn't really help me. There is nothing glorious about being celibate. I certainly don't win the battle in my thought life. It's simply not possible, except in those periods - all too rare - when I am on such a spiritual high that normal sexual desires are diminished somewhat. I don't want to be a martyr. I want to know what it means to love and be loved.

I don't know what I would do if Mr. Right suddenly came riding on a white charger and swept me off my feet, held me and kissed me. I hope I would resist but I can't be certain I would. So I have to substitute by fantasising. And if it is still so hard for me at my age, after more than fifty years as a Christian, and almost fifty as a preacher, what is it like for that young person who has just become a Christian? In demanding that he becomes a super-saint and a martyr overnight you are demanding what you demand of no other Christians.

Only the Roman Catholic Church tells anyone, and then only its priests, that they may not know sex or marry. And that doesn't work as is very well known! It's not something you can demand or legislate. It is a miracle if it happens at all. John McNeill, a Catholic priest who has written a number of books on homosexuality, writes "If priests and religious (meaning someone in religious orders), who attempt a life of chastity under optimum conditions of both nature and grace, are finding it difficult in ever growing numbers, how can we demand such a life from the average homosexual, who shares none of the helps or motivations to be found in clerical or religious life?"

I have to confess that if I were not a minister, with a very strong sense of call by God, I might well have abandoned celibacy years ago. I was once seriously tempted and it was the knowledge that I would lose my ministry, which means everything to me, that stopped me in my tracks. Even then I was not so much worried as to what God would do to me, because I would have believed that he would be gracious with my weaknesses. My worry would have been as to what the church would do to me. It's been done anyway, but too late in life to harm me seriously.

The Consequences of Suppressing Sexuality

McNeill raises another point which many evangelicals probably wouldn't even consider. After years of practising psychotherapy he has come to the conclusion that there are serious consequences for people who spend their lives totally denying or suppressing their sexuality. He makes the statement, in his book *"The Church and the Homosexual"*, "a life of abstinence is not a practical pastoral solution to the problems of lesbian women, and gay men.....I am aware that there are a few exceptional people who have a healthy sexual self-awareness and are capable of genuine intimacy who voluntarily choose a life of sexual abstinence. These people usually feel a call to religious life and ministry and see their life of abstinence as a special grace from God. Their attitude is quite different from those who seek to live out a life of abstinence compulsively because they see their sexual feelings as 'objectively disordered' and any expression of them as 'evil'."

He suggests that the fear of acting wrongly causes Christian gay people to hold back from having any intimate relationship with other people. He avoids getting too close to women because they may misunderstand his intentions. He avoids getting too close to men either because he is scared of rejection, or scared of putting himself in the way of temptation. It causes him to be intensely lonely and often incapable of a healthy social interaction.

I think that by God's Grace I have coped pretty well. I am not sure that my friends who know me well would think the same. There is an awkwardness at times in social situations which I know stems from my homosexuality. I have certainly built barriers around me to prevent people getting too close; and in latter years I have often preferred my own company because it feels so much safer. God made us to be whole people, and sexuality is part of that wholeness and an important part of it. It is inevitable that something will be lacking if we attempt to sublimate or exclude sex from our lives.

Evangelicals tend to see sublimation as a good thing. I'm not so sure of that. John McNeill writes of the traditional approach requiring not only a life of chastity, with no genital sexual relations, "but every expression of warm human affection. Every competent therapist is well aware that all human affection and friendship is normally coloured by a diffused, non-genital form of sexual attraction. Cut off, then, from all deep and affectionate female and male friendship, the homosexual is condemned to a living hell of isolation and loneliness. And such a life is not urged temporarily, but must be sustained until death, under threat of possible eternal damnation". My experience may not be a 'living hell' but I have many compensations and privileges in my life. It is still very difficult.

If we are to make any progress with people in the gay community we are going to have to work with people from where they are. Every situation I have been involved in, where a Christian gay person has been involved in a relationship, or fallen in love for the first time with someone of the same sex, and total abstinence has been demanded - it has led to one thing, their quick exit from the church scene. We are demanding what is virtually impossible, especially if the person is a new Christian or an immature one.

I recently came back from America. I spent some time there with a long-time friend, Richard, who is gay. We did some travelling together and had a lot of time for talking. I first got to know him in 1994 when he was converted to Christ in a gay church where I had just started to work. I was privileged to be involved in discipling him and I have seen him pass through the various stages of his Christian development. For most of the years since 94 he has been in committed relationships, two in fact. In the early years I didn't even suggest he should consider breaking the relationship and become abstinent. It would have put an impossible burden upon him. He was HIV+, and in the days before anti-retrovirals kicked in that meant the expectation of an early death. He was in love with his partner and got immense support from him. He could not have handled a demand that he break up a meaningful and loving relationship, and the important support that was part of it.

From time to time we would discuss my own view of things. I told him that I was committed to be celibate and recommended it as a good ideal to aim for. About three years ago he broke the relationship he was in. But I wasn't entirely sure what this meant. For a while he did try and establish other relationships. But in the last year or so there has been incredible growth in his Christian life. The overused term 'on fire for Christ' would not be inappropriate. He's on such a high spiritually that I can't keep up with him. It is quite clear to me that he is now committed to abstinence at all levels. It remains to be seen whether he will keep it up for the rest of his life. I think he may well succeed. But it is inevitable that he will not remain on the same high as he is on now. He will face temptation again, but because he is now in his middle years, and a strong Christian, there is a good chance he will be able to resist. My point is - it has taken years for him to get to that position.

Acceptance

Last evening I 'bumped into' a younger guy in church who I've known for just a couple of years. He sat next to me. Until fairly recently he had been an active member of another church I am associated with. I asked him why he had left. We sat a long time while he described the hurt and trauma he has gone through. He had an abused childhood, and lots of problems along the way, including a serious motor accident and a battle with epilepsy. He has struggled for a long period of time with his sexual identity. Everybody it seems 'knows' about him, and a lot of people have got involved in trying to 'sort him out', no doubt with good intentions. Unfortunately Christians tend to enjoy doing that.

There is no question he loves God and has been making steady progress in his Christian Life. But he has his lapses. Last year he was without a job, without money to pay his rent, and he lapsed seriously. But it didn't change his love for God and his desire to serve. He is gifted and outgoing. He has proven managerial skills, and he started a house group to win people who struggle like him, in the hope of winning them for Christ. But the people at the church started building barriers around him, no doubt to protect him, but restricting him in his attempts to serve the Lord. He felt not love, acceptance and forgiveness, but censorship - he was a man to be 'watched', a problem guy. He couldn't handle it anymore. His conversion radically changed his life and he's made a lot of progress; but he now feels he will never really be good enough, never really accepted. He will always be a 'special case', different.

I know what he means. He told me that whenever I had preached in his church he had always been blessed. But he said that when he spoke well of my preaching to others, some said "Ah, but there's another side to Graham Ingram". I came home last night feeling down, for him and for myself. Lapses are allowed, and forgotten, for all kinds of things, but if you are gay you will be scrutinised and treated as a special case all your days - or so it seems to me at the moment. Gay people just want to be accepted as ordinary people, not patronised, or treated as the churches 'special project for the new year'.

If we are serious about developing churches that take a compassionate and realistic approach to gay people, we are going to have to learn to live with situations that may fall short of our individual theological and pastoral ideals. All of us who are pastors have had to learn to do that with other issues, and people, we are involved with.

The Circumstantial Will of God

Tony Campolo quotes the views of Lewis Smedes, who until his death a few years ago was professor of theology and ethics at Fuller Theological Seminary, a prestigious evangelical institution. Smedes believed that because we live in a fallen creation nothing is completely the way God intended it to be. Homosexual orientation is one consequence of the Fall, something God did not intend. But we are in an existential situation that we must handle. "He believed" says Campolo "that a committed, life-long, monogamous relationship between homosexuals may be what he would call the 'circumstantial will of God'. Given the circumstances in which gays and lesbians find themselves right now, Smedes, in an address given at the 1998 meeting of Evangelicals Concerned, suggested that a committed relationship in which "couples establish humanising love is the best alternative to the life of celibate loneliness that is often the lot for Christian homosexuals. Smedes drew a parallel by pointing out that, according to Scripture, God's original intention was that every married couple should have children. When he and his wife were not able to do so, they adopted children. This, he believes, was the best decision that they could make, because it enabled him and his wife to live out the 'ultimate will of God', which was to be parents who raised children in the nurture and admonition of the Lord. In a parallel argument, Smedes contended that gay or lesbian marriage is not the original will of God, but it is the circumstantial will of God. This enables the homosexual couple to live out the ultimate will of God, which is to have binding relationships that deliver them from loneliness and enhance the humanity and spirituality of the partners".

Smedes views will not be easily swallowed by most of my readers. But evangelicals need to be able to give an honest answer to what Genesis 2:18 means for gay people, God's statement that "It is not good for the man to be alone. I will make a helper suitable for him." There is no helper, in that sense, for the gay person, or any possibility of one, if intimate same sex relationships are not permissible. *Other single people usually live with that possibility.*

Various attempts are made to solve this problem by individual church families including gay people in their family life. A minister friend of mine has 'adopted' a young man into his family in this way. I admire what he has done. I am not sure that it will work long term. Even though it may help him to live a life of abstinence, gay aspects of his psyche will still be there. He will still have some of the needs of a gay man because they don't begin and end with sex. I spend the great majority of life with straight people, but even if it is only through e-mail contact or visiting gay friends on holiday, I need to be able to relax and talk with other gay folk sometime. Even my best, and most understanding, straight friends tend to get embarrassed if I talk too freely. I resist the temptation to hide away my small collection of stuffed animals when straight friends visit me, but I still find it difficult to be myself. There is unquestionably a 'feminine' side to my make-up.

Churches that want to care for gay folk in the fellowship, will have to consider setting up house groups made up of gay folk, and straight folk who are completely at ease in their company. I've mentioned already a church where I preach in southern California. It would be classified as a 'gay' church, but there are straight members of it who have joined, not just because it is a good spiritual church with good teaching, but because they feel comfortable with gay people and want to identify with them. They are making a statement. There are straight folk in nearly every local church who would enjoy having such a group. This could of course be extended to people actually living in community, although those who've tried this know that it has its own special strains, even when it is made up mainly of heterosexual people.

What about the Detail?

I am conscious that I have not said much as to the 'nuts and bolts' of where we go from here. I have concentrated on attitudes. I don't believe it's possible to lay out a detailed agenda of how a church can bring about change. I've said already that the answers begin at grass roots level, the individual and then the local church. Waiting for the people 'at the top' to give direction may mean waiting a very long time. There is much more at stake at that level. Local situations are much more flexible. But there is also immense variation from one local church to another, as to what is possible.

I want to make a plea. Don't do nothing because you can't swallow a lot of what seems to be in the package. Everyone of us has to be true to his own convictions and conscience. At the same time you should consider you may be sinning if you do nothing.

There is no doubt in my mind that a serious sin has been committed by the Christian church against gay people. Not only because they have been unloved and rejected; and sometimes beaten up and even killed. But also because lies have been spread about them. *One is that there is an equation between being gay and being a paedophile.* There is absolutely no evidence that gay men are more likely to be child molesters than heterosexual men.

Another calumny is the frequent references to 'gay leaders who are pushing a homosexual agenda', as if there was a great plot to take over society. The truth is that if even there were such a plot, gay folk would have a great difficulty implementing it. Gay people are not known for their organisational skills!! Gay people have plenty of sins they need to repent of, most of them the same sins as the rest of humanity. There is a section of the gay community, mainly young people, which is wild, irresponsible and very promiscuous; as is also true of some heterosexual young people. But evangelicals have made homosexuality into a super-sin and homosexuals super-sinners. And so we have helped to create a group of people who are particularly despised by society. If that is changing it is no thanks to us. Of all this we need to repent, not just to God but publicly to gay people. Many churches still have large notice boards outside their building, where sermon titles or scripture texts are displayed. It could do a lot of good to use such a board for a public apology from the church to the gay community.

The Flowering of the Rejects

Years ago I read a book called *"Love, Acceptance and Forgiveness"*. I've lost the book and forgotten the names of the two authors. But I've never forgotten the profound impression it made on me and many of my Christian friends at that time. It described a church that had set out to reach the people other churches didn't want. Some people referred to it as 'the rubbish heap church'. The author described how he had visited the local refuse dump one day, to add some more rubbish of his own; and found a lovely flower growing out of the rubbish.

That spoke to me powerfully. Soon afterwards I was involved in starting a new church in which we had freedom to develop new ideas, new forms of worship, and new attitudes to people. The Charismatic renewal was bringing many new churches into being; churches in which grace was not just a doctrine but an experience and a lifestyle. Some critics began to refer to it as 'the Grace Place', inferring that we had taken it too far and were soft on sin. We had no stated policy in dealing with gay people, and I now realise that many joined us. We were often unaware of how many, because we just treated them, like everyone else, as people needing Christ, needing to be loved and shown grace. For the most part it wasn't an issue. I am sure that as they grew in Christ they were able cope better with the demands of discipleship.

But in later years, after I left the church, new leaders began a 'clean up process'. Graham Ingram had been 'too soft on sin'. Soon there were wounded sheep running in all directions. I know because I had to help some of them. One or two gay people were given a particularly hard time. The vision of what the church should be had gone. The old Pharasaism and legalism has begun to return in many of the new churches, as well as the old. Autocratic leaders enjoy flexing their muscles, and who better to flex them on than despised gay people.

When it comes down to it, few Christians really want to mix with the outcasts, as Jesus did. We want our churches to be places where middle class values reign, and our respectability shines for all to see. Soon after I moved to LA in 1994 I began to get bombarded with letters from friends who thought I had made a terrible mistake. I went to visit a minister friend who was pastoring with the Vineyard movement in Malibu. I wanted him to act as a check on what I was doing. The incident is described in chapter two. I asked him to be honest and tell me if he thought I was acting wrongly. He listened to my story and at the end expressed his general support for what I was doing.

He went on to tell me that John Wimber, the founder of the Vineyard churches, had once said that he thought it was likely that God was going to do something special in the gay community. He compared it to the move of the Spirit in the seventies, often referred to as the Jesus movement, in which large numbers of young people in California had come to Christ. They had been non-church types; surfers and hippies. The Vineyard churches, and some other groups, emerged out of that revival. By and large traditional churches could not cope with their unconventional lifestyles. It needed new wineskins to cope with the new wine. Wimber felt that the next such move of God could be in the gay community.

Just as Jesus went to the despised, in part to shame the false religious leaders of his day, sometimes God does that to shake up the complacency of his church. It was like that in the eighteenth century revival in England, when George Whitefield went to the pit heads to preach to coal miners and he and Wesley preached to large crowds of poor and ignorant folk in the open air, because the churches had no room for such people.

Who knows whether God may stir up a generation of heterosexual young Christians, as well as gay Christians, with a vision to win gay folk for Christ; folk who are willing to go and live in the gay ghettos, visit the gay bars and clubs, in order to identify with and love gay people. What if God should bless their efforts, and there should be a new wave of the Spirit? Would traditional Evangelical and Charismatic churches rejoice in it?

I am not sure they all would. They would be uneasy in letting the Spirit work in his own way in forming Christ's character in these gay people who had responded to the Gospel, just as the churches of the seventies wanted the Jesus people to get their hair cut and dress properly, and stop smoking pot, before they were welcome. Maybe there would have to be a new wave of church planting in which relevant wineskins would come into being, not as 'gay churches' but as churches where gay people and straight people could fellowship together and work together, not just to reach gay people for Christ but all the rejects of society, the people who don't fit easily into traditional evangelical structures.

If we don't listen to God, and don't open our hearts, God may pass us by.

FOR FURTHER READING

Helpful Books by evangelical authors on homosexuality

Hopper, George: *Reluctant Journey* – published by the author 1997

Vasey, Michael: *Strangers & Friends* – Hodder & Stoughton 1995

White, Mel: *Stranger at the Gate* – Plume Books 1994

Helpful Books by evangelical authors which refer to homosexuality

Campolo, Tony: *Was Jesus a Moderate?* – Word Publishing 2005

Campolo, Tony: *Speaking my Mind* – Word Publishing 2005

Wallis, Jim: *God's Politics* – Harper 2005

Yancey, Philip: *What's so Amazing about Grace?* – Zondervan 1997

Useful Books by non-evangelical authors referred to in the text

Fortress Press: *The New Testament and Homosexuality* – 1984

McNeill, Fr John: *The Church and the Homosexual* – Beach Press 1983

Highly recommended:

A series of articles on *What makes people gay?* Published over a number of weeks in the Boston Globe:

www.boston.com/news/globe/magazine/articles/2005/08/14/wh at_makes_people_gay/?

APPENDIX

THREE STUDIES FOR HOME GROUPS

Brief Note for Leaders: Please do not try and answer all the questions as they stand: this is not an examination! You know your group and your church, and we do not, so we set out below some ideas to get you started: they are simply signposts to suggest some interesting directions. Please try and end with a time of group prayer, drawing together the key insights you have shared.

Graham's concern is that Christian gay people should feel welcomed and accepted in our churches, but sometimes without thinking we say and do things that are deeply hurtful. Our hope and prayer is that through these studies a sincere and genuine love will grow in our churches not only for gay people but for all who feel marginalised and excluded.

WEEK 1:   Chapters 1-5:   Gay People We Know

If possible, ask people to think about gay people they know before they start reading the book. If they are willing, ask them to list them, and put a few notes down about how they feel about them. If there are any in the church, ask the group to think about how they feel they relate to them as fellow Christians. If there are none in the church, ask people to list down some reasons why they think this is so.

Then ask people to read the first five chapters and review their notes. Has anything they have read caused them to re-evaluate anything?

1.1   Definitions: is the group clear on exactly what we are talking about? What words will we use in our discussions, and what will we agree that they mean?

1.2   Is there sometimes confusion in our discussions on gay issues because of definitions?

1.3   Think of the gay people you know: are there common threads, or is the variety too large to stereotype?

1.4   Why do you think some people are gay but most are not?

1.5   Is it simply 'either/or' or is there a spectrum of inclination?

1.6   Do you believe that gay people chose to be gay?

1.7   What do you understand by a 'gay lifestyle'?

1.8   How do you feel about people you work with who have a gay lifestyle? If you do not work with any such person, how do you think you would feel if your next boss was a person with a gay lifestyle?

1.9   Do you think that gay issues can be properly compared with slavery issues and the ordination of women?

1.10 In what ways is the church called to change in each generation?

1.11 How do you know if somebody is filled with the Holy Spirit? Would your answer be any different for a gay person?

1.12 Would you be concerned if the church proposed to appoint a gay person to lead the Sunday School?

Prayer: John 15:12 *Love one another as I have loved you.*

WEEK 2: Chapter 6: Interpreting the Verses

You may like to read the key verses in a variety of translations, and you might like to research beforehand how many different translations you can find:

> Genesis 18:26 and 19:29; Leviticus 18:22 and 20:13; I Corinthians 6:9-11; Romans 1:26-29

2.1   What clear messages can you all agree from these verses?

2.2   Can you think of any relevant passages in the Gospels that might be appropriate to this discussion?

2.3   What did you agree with in Chapter 6 and what did you disagree with?

2.4   How would you now state your position on controversial gay issues in the light of what you believe is the correct interpretation of these verses?

2.5   Could you enjoy full Christian fellowship with somebody who disagreed with your view?

2.6   Women often have close female friends and this is quite acceptable, but for men to have close male friends is somehow seen to be questionable. Why do you think this is so? Should Christian men work to change this view, perhaps by setting an example?

2.7   How far should Christian leaders go in establishing what sort of sexual activity is taking place between adults in their churches?

2.8   Do you think the church has often given more attention to sexual sins than to other types of sin? If so, is this attention justified?

2.9 Genesis 2:18: how do you believe God intended those with a homosexual orientation to be companioned?

2.10 Overall, has the Roman Catholic Church been blessed because of its views on the celibacy of its priests?

2.11 What choices would you set out for a school teenager in the church youth group who confides in you that he thinks he might be gay? Would your answer be different if you were aware that the rest of the youth group were already aware of this possibility? How would your answer differ if the person was a university student?

2.12 In this whole debate, what one question would you really like to ask Jesus? How do you think he would answer it?

Prayer:

Matthew 7:1-5 *Do not judge, so that you may not be judged. For with the judgment you make you will be judged, and the measure you give will be the measure you get. Why do you see the speck in your neighbour's eye, but do not notice the log in your own eye? Or how can you say to your neighbour, "Let me take the speck out of your eye", while the log is in your own eye? You hypocrite, first take the log out of your own eye, and then you will see clearly to take the speck our of your neighbour's eye.*

Are we comfortable coming to God in prayer having had our discussion and considered these words of Jesus?

Let us pray for clear vision and spiritual wisdom, both for ourselves and for leaders in the church.

WEEK 3: Chapters 7 & 8: How welcome are Gay People in our Church?

Before you start this final session, you might ask each person to summarise where they are at this point: have their views been hardened or changed, and what are those views?

3.1   What are the views of your Church Leadership Team on gay issues?

3.2   Do you agree with them? Are there some areas where you think more work should be done?

3.3   What differences are there now in the way parents and children talk about sex with the way they talked forty years ago? Are these same differences true in the church?

3.4   "Start with the Real, Work to the Ideal": do you agree with this? To what Bible passages would you point to justify your answer?

3.5   Is losing a relationship with a gay child part of the cross that some Christian disciples are called to bear?

3.6   What are the limits of love? Is there a difference between the limits of parental love and the limits of the love that Jesus calls his disciples to have for their neighbours?

3.7   Should forgiveness be conditional on repentance? What Bible passages would you point to?

3.8   Where there is a broken relationship, what does the call of Jesus to 'love our neighbour as ourself' mean? Does 'neighbour' exclude child and partner? Does 'neighbour' include the recently released paedophile next door?

3.9   What do you aim for in loving someone with whom you profoundly disagree?

3.10   What are the principles you apply when deciding who to give time to?

3.11   Look up Lonnie Frisbee on the internet; you might like to get hold of the video of his life in the Jesus Movement, Calvary Chapel and the Vineyard. If you were told that one of the people who was instrumental in helping you to faith was dying of AIDS, what would be your immediate reaction?

3.12   A gay couple in a civil partnership join an Alpha Course you are running: set out for your co-leader how you think you should both handle this. What will you do if one is clearly filled with the Spirit on the weekend away but the other is not?

Prayer:

Luke 14:21 *Then the owner of the house became angry and said to his slave, "Go out at once into the streets and lanes of the town and bring in the poor, the crippled, the blind, and the lame." And the slave said, "Sir, what you have ordered has been done, and there is still room." Then the master said to the slave, "Go out into the roads and lanes, and compel people to come in, so that my house may be filled. For I tell you, none of those who were invited will taste my dinner."*

Let us pray that the joy of the Kingdom may be ours here and now as we celebrate with all those who know the risen Jesus and try to follow him day by day in the power of the Holy Spirit.